Bible Principles
of
Interpretation

Louis F. Were

BIBLE PRINCIPLES OF INTERPRETATION

Establish Truth and Safeguard Against Last-Day Errors

By Louis F. Were

© 2008 by Laymen Ministries

ISBN: 978-0-9665786-7-6

Published by:

Laymen Ministries

414 Zapada Rd.
St. Maries, ID 83861

The references in this edition have been carefully checked, and as a result, may differ slightly in some cases from the original text. Every effort has been made to ensure that all references are accurate.

FOREWORD

Many a portion of Scripture which learned men pronounce a mystery, or pass over as unimportant, is full of comfort and instruction to him who has been taught in the school of Christ" (GC 599).

"We can attain to an understanding of God's Word only through the illumination of that Spirit by which the Word was given . . . . If we would not have the Scriptures clouded to our understanding, . . . we must have the simplicity and faith of a little child, ready to learn, and beseeching the aid of the Holy Spirit . . . . There are many things apparently difficult or obscure, which God will make plain and simple to those who thus seek an understanding of them" (SC 109).

"The idea that certain portions of the Bible can not be understood has led to neglect of some of its most important truths.... The mysteries of the Bible are not such because God has sought to conceal truth, but because our own weakness or ignorance makes us incapable of comprehending or appropriating truth. The limitation is not in its purpose, but in our capacity. Of those very portions of Scripture so often passed by as impossible to be understood, God desires us to understand as much as our minds are capable of receiving" (ST, April 25, 1906).

CONTENTS

KEY TO ABBREVIATIONS

1T, 2T, etc. . . . . *Testimonies,* Vol. 1, Vol. 2, etc.

AA . . . . *The Acts of the Apostles*

1BC, 2BC, etc. . . . *SDA Bible Commentary,* Vol. 1, Vol. 2, etc.

COL. . . . . *Christ's Object Lessons*

CT. . . . . *Counsels to Parents, Teachers, and Students*

DA . . . . *The Desire of Ages*

Ed . . . . *Education*

Ev . . . . *Evangelism*

EW . . . . *Early Writings*

FE . . . . *Fundamentals of Christian Education*

GC . . . . *The Great Controversy*

GW . . . . *Gospel Workers*

LS . . . . *Life Sketches, New Edition*

MB . . . . *Thoughts From the Mount of Blessing*

MH . . . . *Ministry of Healing*

MM. . . . . *Medical Ministry*

Ms. 1, Ms. 2, etc. . . . *Manuscript No. 1, No. 2, etc.*

PK . . . . *Prophets and Kings*

PP . . . . *Patriarchs and Prophets*

RH . . . . *Review & Herald Articles*

SC . . . . *Steps to Christ*

ST . . . . *Signs of the Times Articles*

TM . . . . *Testimonies to Ministers*

*Note: Emphasis to extracts employed has been added to draw attention to certain salient features.

Other referenced publications, such as *Thoughts on Daniel and Revelation,* may no longer be in print, or may be a different edition than is currently in print.

PROLOGUE

THE CERTAINTY OF OUR MESSAGE

I t is as certain that we have the truth as that God lives" (4T 595). We "ought not to guess at anything" (GC 598). How did the pioneers of our Movement obtain the advanced understanding of the Word of God? "We would search the Scriptures with much prayer. . . . Sometimes whole nights would be devoted to searching the Scriptures, and earnestly asking God for guidance" (GW 302). "We are to repeat the words of the pioneers in our work, who knew what it cost to search for the truth as for hidden treasure" (RH, May 25, 1905).

God's last-day Message is so fully established upon principles of interpretation that by these we can prove it to be of God.

"I saw that the Word of God, as a whole, is a perfect chain, one portion linking into and explaining another" (EW 221). Any misinterpretation will break the "perfect chain."

"Knowing this first, that no prophecy of the Scripture is of any *private interpretation*. For prophecy came not in old time by the will of man: but holy men of God spake [as they were] moved by the Holy Ghost" (2 Pet. 1:20, 21). Prophecies given by the Holy Spirit must be explained by the Holy Spirit. "He shall teach you all things" (John 14:26). "When He, the Spirit of truth, is come, He will guide you into all truth" (John 16:13). Paul declared that he was taught by the Holy Spirit: "Which things also we speak, not in the words which man's wisdom teacheth, but which the Holy Ghost teacheth; *comparing spiritual things with spiritual*. But the natural man receiveth not the things of the Spirit of God: for they are foolishness unto him … because they are *spiritually discerned*" (1 Cor. 2:13, 14). The Holy

Spirit taught him by guiding him to compare one Scripture with another: one verse not being sufficient on its own; rather, much study being required to bring together the links in the chain of truth. This procedure is not acceptable to "the natural man." The more we yield to the Spirit's guidance the more we will—like the Pioneers of our Movement—employ this method of ascertaining the "perfect chain" of truth to be found in the Scriptures, and the less we will rely upon the method of "the natural man" in merely reading a verse and giving his opinion of it. "We should make the Bible its own expositor" (TM 106). "Compare Scripture with Scripture" (TM 476). "The Bible is its own expositor. Scripture is to be compared with Scripture" (Ed 190). "The Bible is its own interpreter, one passage explaining another" (4T 499).

THE UNIVERSALITY OF LAW

1. Laws of Science help scientific comprehension.

2. Laws of Nature must be studied to learn the secrets of nature.

3. Laws of Health are an essential study for healthful living.

4. Laws of interpretation are infallible tests in studying Bible prophecies.

"There are great laws that govern the world of nature, and spiritual things are controlled by principles equally certain" (9T 221).

'GOD IS NOT THE AUTHOR OF CONFUSION'
(1 Cor. 14:33)

"System and order are manifest in all the works of God throughout the universe. Order is the law of Heaven. . . . Everything connected with Heaven is in perfect order" (TM 26, 29).

Everything in nature is governed by laws or principles. Chemists, scientists working in all branches of natural research, discover the laws with which God has endowed nature: the principles by which the Creator sustains His vast and complicated creation. Success comes as we discover and use the laws of God in the natural world: failure comes through a disregard of these laws. As never before, men now see that everything in nature is controlled by certain laws or principles. As the Bible has been inspired by God (2 Tim. 3:16; 2 Pet. 1:21, etc.), is it not reasonable to believe that the Scriptures are based upon definite laws of interpretation which we must study and follow if we would obtain a true understanding of the Word of God? How are the laws of nature discovered? By patient research. Similarly, he who patiently and prayerfully searches the Scriptures, learns from his *"study"* that there are laws which govern in *"rightly dividing* the Word of truth." "Thou hast magnified Thy Word above all Thy name" (Ps. 138:2). Thus we should expect to find that laws or principles of interpretation operate in the study of God's Word. As scientists have opened up many realms through discovering and applying the laws which operate throughout nature, so will we make important discoveries from God's mine of truth if we heed the laws of interpretation. GOD'S WORD MUST BE RIGHTLY DIVIDED—this requires effort, patience.

"Study to show thyself approved unto God, a *workman* that needeth not to be ashamed, *rightly dividing* the Word of truth" (2 Tim. 2:15).

"So the finder of heavenly treasure will count no labor too great and no sacrifice too dear, in order to gain the treasures of truth. In the parable the field containing the treasure represents the Holy Scriptures. . . . In *types* and *symbols* the great truths of redemption were veiled." Men are "too indolent to put themselves to diligent, earnest labor, represented in the Word as digging for hidden treasure." "Christ's words are truth, and they have a deeper significance than appears on the surface. . . . There must be earnest study and close investigation. Sharp, clear perceptions of truth will never be the reward of indolence. . . . We cannot expect to gain spiritual knowledge without earnest toil. Those who desire to find the treasures of truth must dig for them as the miner digs for treasure hidden in the earth" (COL 104-114).

Many principles to guide us in our study are presented in the Scriptures, but as our outline must be limited in size, we will present only those which, when applied, prove that our message is indeed God's last-day Message—"That thou mightest know the certainty of those things, wherein thou hast been instructed" (Luke 1:4; Prov. 22:21).

BIBLE PRINCIPLES OF INTERPRETATION PROVED AND APPLIED IN THE STUDY OF LAST-DAY PROPHECIES

PRINCIPLE ONE:
The Interpretation Must Reveal Christ and Make Him the Center

S earch the Scriptures . . . they are they that testify of Me" (John 5:39).

"The whole Bible tells of Christ. From the first record of creation . . . to the closing promise we are reading of His works and listening to His voice" (SC 88).

Application:

The Apocalypse is "the Revelation of Jesus Christ" (Rev. 1:1); "I Jesus have sent Mine angel to testify unto you these things in the churches" (Rev. 22:16). In Rev. 16:15 (in the description of events under the 6th plague) the Lord's use of the personal pronoun "I" is significant, for He speaks thus when the message He gives is of the *utmost importance*—see examples: Ex. 20:2; note "but *I* say unto you" in the "Sermon on the Mount"; observe the Lord's use of "I" in Isa. 41:4, 10, 13, 25; 42:1, 6, 8, 14, 15; 43:1, 2, 3, 4, 5, 6, 7, etc. Scores of times "I" is employed in these chapters wherein our Lord spoke of His love for His people, and reminded them of His almighty power that He, the Creator, would employ for their deliverance from their enemies. He used "I" over 100 times on the evening of His betrayal as He counseled so earnestly with His disciples. In the Revelation Jesus employed the "I" when addressing His people personally on matters which He deemed most vital for them. On the first occasion (Rev. 1:8) He declared He was the Almighty, the Creator. In the first three chapters our Lord speaks often with the personal pronoun "I" concerning His inherent position as a member of the Godhead, His resurrection, His power over death, His infinite knowledge of all that pertains to the seven churches. In Rev. 4:1 He declares that He knows all the future. He does not use "I" again until Rev. 11:3, where He comforted His people, saying that He had permitted the papal persecution. He does not employ the "I" again until Rev. 16:15. As He comforted His people who suffered for Him during Papal persecution with the personal pronoun "I," so He comforts His remnant people that it is all permitted for a wise purpose, and assures them that He will exercise His almighty power on their behalf.

But, it should be pointed out, how does the interpretation that Rev. 16:12-16 envisages a military war reveal Christ? What has been given by some as the reason for the supposed literal gathering to Palestine?—the minerals of the Dead Sea, or the oil wells of the Middle East, etc. Such human guesses convey no revelation of Jesus Christ, they only display human ingenuity; and confuse the Message Christ has sought to convey, causing some to say that this prophecy is not important, which reflects upon the wisdom of God in giving it: "Every chapter and every verse of the Bible is a communication from God to man" (PP 504). "Do we receive the Bible as the 'oracle of God'? It is as really a Divine communication as though its words came to us in an audible voice" (5T 533).

The True Interpretation Makes Christ the Center:

"Christ, the great center from which radiates all glory" (TM 19).

"Christ is the center of all true doctrine" (CT 453).

"Every true doctrine makes Christ the center" (6T 54).

Application:

In all last-day prophecies describing the final conflict, Jerusalem is pictured as being the center, see Dan. 11:45; Joel 2:32 and chapter 3; Zech. 14; Rev. 14:1; 16:12-16, etc. By interpreting these prophecies as referring to the literal city of Jerusalem the interpretation is shown to be incorrect, for Christ is not reigning in literal Jerusalem: "Every true doctrine makes Christ the center" (6T 54). "The curse is upon Old Jerusalem" (RH, Feb. 25, 1896); "The curse of God is upon Jerusalem" (RH, June 9, 1896). Christ is "the center"—not the Papacy or Turkey—reigning in "the glorious holy mountain." It is "holy" because He is there. The prophecy of Zech. 2 pictures God reigning in "Jerusalem," and the Spirit of Prophecy in commenting upon it says: " . . .*Christ, the great center* from which radiates all glory" (TM 15-19).

PRINCIPLE TWO:
Compare Scripture With Scripture for Clearer Light

C ompare spiritual things with spiritual" (1 Cor. 2:13).

"Here a little, there a little" (Isa. 28:10, 13).

"The prophets have inquired and searched diligently. . . . Searching what, or what manner of time the Spirit of Christ did signify when It testified beforehand the sufferings of Christ, and the glory that should follow" (1 Pet. 1:10, 11; see Dan. 8:27; 9:2; etc.).

"I saw that the Word of God, as a whole, is a perfect chain, one portion linking into and explaining another" (EW 221).

"Scripture is explained by Scripture" (1SM 42).

"The illuminated soul sees a spiritual unity, one grand golden thread running through the whole, but it requires patience, thought, and prayer to trace out the precious golden thread" (1SM 20).

"The Bible is its own expositor. Scripture is to be compared with Scripture. The student should learn to view the Word as a whole, and to see the relation of its parts" (Ed 190; CT 462).

"Its [the Bible's] great system of truth is not so presented as to be discerned by the hasty or careless reader. Many of its treasures lie far beneath the surface, and can be obtained only by diligent research and continuous effort. The truths that go to make up the great whole must be searched out and gathered up, 'here a little, and there a little' (Isa. 28:10). When thus searched out and brought together, they will be found to be perfectly fitted to one another. Each Gospel is a supplement to the others, every prophecy an explanation of another, every truth a development of some other truth" (Ed 123, 124).

"Investigate, compare Scripture with Scripture, sink the shaft of truth deep into the mine of God's Word" (TM 476).

"We should make the Bible its own expositor" (TM 106).

"When he [Miller] found anything obscure, it was his custom to compare it with every other text which seemed to have any reference to the matter under consideration . . . if his view of it harmonized with every collateral passage, it ceased to be a difficulty. Thus whenever he met with a passage hard to be understood he found an explanation in some other portion of the Scriptures" (GC 320).

One of the main proofs that the Bible is indeed the Word of God, that men separated from other men in time or by distance were moved by the Holy Spirit, is that various parts of the Bible, though written at different times and in different countries, fit together perfectly. It is this that inspires confidence in God and His Word. The Lord's servant says: "The Bible is its own interpreter, one passage explaining another. By comparing Scriptures referring to the same subjects, you will see beauty and harmony of which you have never dreamed" (4T 499).

A simple illustration shows the necessity of comparing parallel passages in order to obtain the full light on a given subject. Compare the record given in each Gospel of the wording of the title on the Cross:

Matt. 27:37: "THIS IS JESUS THE KING OF THE JEWS."

Mark 15:26: "THE KING OF THE JEWS."

Luke 23:38: "THIS IS THE KING OF THE JEWS."

John 19:19: "JESUS OF NAZARETH THE KING OF THE JEWS."

Thus we ascertain the complete title on the cross: "THIS IS JESUS OF NAZARETH THE KING OF THE JEWS." This principle may be discerned throughout the Bible. The Holy Spirit inspired each man to write his particular portion as part of an overall pattern, which would not be known to them, for those who wrote the earlier portions had no way of knowing that others would later be inspired to write, nor would they know what later prophets would write. Thus the more the Scriptures are compared with each other and the more completed pictures of truth are discerned, the more it becomes evident that only an infinite Mind could have inspired a number of men of various times and countries to write a Book with such "beauty and harmony." By bringing together through studying, searching, and learning to rightly divide the Word of truth, one becomes convinced that God's Spirit did indeed superintend the writing of this Holy Mosaic of inspiration. The Holy Spirit, the Author of this amazing Book, as an infallible Artist, used each man to dip his brush in the required colors and place on the canvas of thought his distinctive color. Until, and not until, the last man applied his color was the picture perfected. Today, we, through the Spirit of Prophecy, have been especially blessed in being able to see more of the wonderful harmony, the matchless blending of the color scheme of Inspiration. Certain interpretations given of some prophecies of Holy Writ have not been derived by heeding the heavenly counsel of comparing Scripture with Scripture, thus they have hid some of the "beauty and harmony."

Application to last-day prophecies:

If it were possible for a doubt as to whether Dan. 11:45 referred to the literal Jerusalem, comparison with other texts such as Joel 2:32; 3:17, etc., should easily show that it could not possibly refer to the literal Jerusalem, because such an application would throw it out of harmony with other prophecies mentioning Jerusalem, which are applied as meaning the Church. The gathering of Gog's armies against Israel in Israel's land could not refer to the Russians attacking the literal Jews in Palestine, for that would violate the principle that Israel in the New Testament is the word employed for the Church; it would also violate the New Testament "spiritual" application of Old Testament prophecies in which Palestinian geography is mentioned. In Rev. 20:8, Gog is employed as a designation for the enemies of God and His people. To apply Gog to Russia as the enemies of literal Jews in Palestine would throw the prophecy of Ezek. 38, 39 out of harmony with Rev. 20:8, and the rest of the New Testament.

In the Old Testament, the river Euphrates is repeatedly stated to be the boundary of the land of Israel: Gen. 15:18; Deut. 1:7; 2 Kings 23:29; 24:7; 1 Chron. 18:3, etc. It represented the power of Babylon (Jer. 13:4-9, 20; 46:1-6;

50:38; 51:13, etc.) Its overflowing represented the invasion of the land of Israel by their enemies, see Isa. 8:7, 8. God called "Abram *the Hebrew*" from the region beyond the Euphrates, as that word "Hebrew" indicates. God's remnant, like Abraham their "father," are also *"Hebrews"* who have come out of Babylon, from beyond the Euphrates. We know, therefore, that the Euphrates mentioned in Rev. 16:12 has an *Israel* or *Church* setting: it could not refer to anything else, especially in the setting in which it occurs—depicting the doom of Babylon out of which the remnant have come.

A *Commentary of the New Testament* says: "We must remember that throughout this book *Canaan represents the locality of the Church of God.*" Ellicott's *Commentary on Revelation*, pp. 127, 128, 195, says: "*The whole tenor* of the Apocalypse *keeps before us Jerusalem, the temple, and its surroundings, and Babylon.* . . . The inconsistency and arbitrariness of interpreters is tested by these three names, Babylon, Jerusalem, Euphrates. . . . It is in this war between the mystical Jerusalem and the mystical Babylon that the great river Euphrates is to play an important part. . . . Babylon is the great foe of Israel, and the Euphrates was the great river or flood which formed a natural boundary between them."

By comparing Old Testament passages mentioning Euphrates, we know that the Euphrates in Rev. 16:12 could not possibly refer to any local nation such as Turkey, etc., but is used as a symbol of the worldwide power of Babylon invading the land of Israel. Her armies were destroyed, as were the Assyrians whose invading armies were likened to waters of the Euphrates flooding across the land of Emmanuel, see Isa. 8:7, 8; 37:33, 36.

There is a Scriptural law of the First and the Last, which space prevents us dealing with in this outline, and by it we compare the first conflict fought at Megiddo with the last (Rev. 16:16). In the first, sun-worshipping Canaanites (Judg. 5:19-21) fought against Israel, but God gave Israel the victory. All their enemies were destroyed: "And there was not a man left" (4:16). In the last, spiritual Israel's enemies, endeavoring to enforce the day anciently dedicated to the sun, seek to slay them, but they, instead, are all slain at "Armageddon."

PRINCIPLE THREE:
The Things of Israel Now Belong to the Church

This principle is positively fundamental to the understanding of the prophecies of Daniel and the Revelation—it is the foundational principle of God's last-day Message. The Lord gave Paul the special commission of showing how the church became "the Israel of God," that the promises to literal Israel were to be fulfilled in the experiences of the church:

"They which are the children of the flesh, these are *not* the children of God: but the children of the promise are *counted* for the seed" (Rom. 9:6-8). "*If ye be Christ's,* then are ye Abraham's seed, and heirs according to the promise"; "*They which are of faith,* the same are the children of Abraham" (Gal. 3:29, 7). "We, brethren, as Isaac was, are the children of promise" (Gal. 3:29, 7; 4:28). People previously classified as "Gentiles" become "fellow citizens of the saints" in "the commonwealth of Israel" (Eph. 2:12-22; 1 Pet. 2:10, etc.). This is the consistent teaching of all the New Testament (after the rejection of national Israel).

"*We* are numbered with Israel . . . *all* the promises of blessing through obedience are *for us*" (MH 405). "I was also shown that those who are trying to obey God . . . are God's chosen people, *His modern Israel*" (2T 108, 109). "The Israel of today . . . the true church of Christ"; ". . . spiritual Israel—His church on earth" (PK 74, 370-372). The principle that Israel's history is typical or prophetical of the experiences of the church is continually employed in the Spirit of Prophecy.

The Application of the principle that the things of Israel now belong to the church is vital to the understanding of the Revelation in general and "Armageddon" in particular. It should be remembered that the New Testament, when speaking of the church, employs the same terminology as the Old Testament: kingdom, nation, Israel, temple, Jerusalem, Zion, tribes of Israel, etc. When Jesus spoke of the church, which takes the place of national Israel, He said: "The *kingdom* of God shall be taken from you [*literal* Israel], and given to a *nation* [*spiritual* Israel] bringing forth the fruits thereof" (Matt. 21:43). "Ye (the church) are . . . a holy *nation*" (1 Pet. 2:9). While Old Testament language is employed in the New Testament when referring to the church, the same phraseology is *spiritualized* and applied in a *worldwide* sense. These terms are not prefaced with the word *"spiritual"* because other plain statements clearly state that the church has taken the place of literal Israel. Having made it clear that national Israel was rejected of God, that "wrath is come upon them to the uttermost" (1 Thess. 2:16), it was needless to say that the *same* terminology in the New Testament now meant the worldwide church; that was self-evident. Similarly when studying the Revelation—the "Israel" setting must be regarded as referring to the church. However, so often when speaking of last-day events, expositors have failed to apply the New Testament principle. Because of the "Israel" imagery so abundantly used in the Revelation, futurists say that it is a book largely pertaining to the literal Jew in Palestine.

"Israel" is the key which unlocks prophetic problems—especially those in the Revelation. Many commentators have rightly emphasized that "the symbolism of the Revelation is *wholly and exclusively Jewish.*" As stated in *Elliott's Commentary, Notes on Revelation*: "The Christian Church absorbs the Jewish, inherits her privileges, and adopts, with wider and nobler meaning *her phraseology*" (p. 96); "The historical basis of the Apocalypse is the past history of the chosen people. . . . The Apocalypse shows us the principle working in the highest levels and in a wide arena. The Israel of God, the church of Christ, *takes the place of the national Israel*" (p. 125). Dr. W. Milligan says: "The Book is absolutely steeped in the memories, incidents, the thoughts, and the language of the church's past. To such an extent is this the case that it may be *doubted whether it contains a single figure not drawn from the Old Testament, or a single sentence not more or less built up of materials from the same source* . . . a perfect mosaic of passages from the Old Testament

. . . there is to be found nowhere else such a perfect fusion of the revelation given to Israel with the mind of one who would either express Israel's ideas, or give utterance, by means of the symbols supplied by Israel's history, to the purest and most elevated thoughts of the Christian faith." Bishop C. Wordsworth wrote: "The diction of the Book of Revelation is *more Hebraistic than that of any other portion of the New Testament . . . spiritualizing* the language of the Jewish nation."

The prophecies of the Apocalypse can be understood only when interpreted in relation to the church. Only spiritual Israelites can understand the meaning of the destruction of the enemies of the church at "a place called in the *Hebrew* tongue Armageddon." To interpret "Armageddon" without making the church the center of it reveals a failure to grasp the underlying principle of God's last-day Message, which is that the church is Israel *pictured* as dwelling in the land of Israel. The believers have "come out" of Babylon to Mt. Sion and have taken their stand "with Him" there (Rev. 14:1). The "nations rage and imagine a vain thing"—they plan to destroy God's people. Instead, they themselves are destroyed "in the battle of that great day of God Almighty" (Ps. 2; Rev. 16:12-16; 17:14-17, 18; 19:11-21). They will "fall upon the mountains *of Israel*" and be buried in a "*place . . . in Israel*" (Ezek. 39:4, 11)—the geography mentioned locates this "*place*" as Megiddo, a word which comes from a Hebrew root "gadad," meaning "to cut off, slaughter." The Revelator's reference to this "*place*" and all that pertains to this graphic picture of "Armageddon" can be understood only as a symbolic presentation of the final conflict when the powers of earth combine in an attempt to destroy "the Israel of God."

PRINCIPLE FOUR:
The Gospel in Every Passage and Prophecy

*A*ll Scripture" is given by God "for instruction in righteousness" (2 Tim. 3:15, 16).

"The burden of *every* book and *every* passage of the Bible is the unfolding of this wondrous theme—man's uplifting—the power of God, 'which giveth us the victory through our Lord Jesus Christ' (1 Cor. 15:57). He who grasps this thought has before him an infinite field for study. He has the *key* that will unlock to him the whole treasure-house of God's Word" (Ed 125, 126).

The Application:

What of some passages and prophecies where "instruction in righteousness" does not appear to be present? From the foregoing principles we know that, by comparing these portions with others and digging more deeply, we shall find that they often contain most important "instruction in righteousness." We take a couple of prophecies which are regarded by some as having nothing to do with salvation.

Where is the Gospel proclaimed in the 7 Trumpets (Rev. 8, 9)? In the fact that Christ sends judgments upon the enemies of His people in answer to their prayers—for this reason the study of the 7 Trumpets is introduced in connection with a description of the prayer altar and the prayers of God's people ascending as sweet incense because commingled with the righteousness of Christ (vs. 2-5). The reference to the prayer altar and the prayers of God's people ascending to God concludes with the words: "And there were voices, and thunderings, and lightnings, and an earthquake." These point to the events under the 7th plague, concerning which we read: "And the 7th angel poured out his vial into the air; and there came a great voice out of the temple of heaven, from the throne, saying, It is done. And there were voices, and thunders, and lightnings; and there was a great earthquake. . . . And the great city [Babylon] was divided into three parts, and the cities of the nations fell: and great Babylon came in remembrance before God, to give unto her the cup of the wine of the fierceness of His wrath" (Rev. 16:17-19). We know positively that God's voice, saying "It is done," delivers His people from their enemies: "Then all the saints cried out with anguish of spirit, and were *delivered by the voice of God*" (EW 37). "The captivity of the righteous is turned, and with sweet and solemn whisperings they say one to one another, 'We are delivered. It is the voice of God.' . . . Satan and evil angels flee from the presence of the saints glorified. *Their power to annoy them is gone forever*" (1T 354). "There have been conflicts, and there will be *until* in heaven *the voice of the Lord is heard, saying, `It is done'*" (RH, Oct. 13, 1904 and July 12, 1945). See also GC 636; EW 284. "We are told of a greater battle to take place in the closing scenes of earth's history, when 'Jehovah hath opened His armory, and hath brought forth the weapons of His indignation' (Jer. 50:25). . . . The Revelator describes the *destruction* that is to take place *when* the 'great voice out of the temple of heaven' announces, 'It is done'" (PP 509).

Thus we know that both the 7 Trumpets and the 7 Plagues have to do with the judgments which God sends upon the persecutors of His people, for He answers their prayers and brings them deliverance. This principle has always operated: "The righteous cry, and the Lord heareth, and delivereth them out of all their troubles" (Ps. 34:17). As God sent plagues upon the Egyptians because of their persecution of His people, so He will send the 7 last plagues upon those who are persecuting His people. Concerning this we are definitely informed: "God's judgments will be visited upon those who are seeking to oppress and destroy His people. . . . The plagues upon Egypt when God was about to *deliver* Israel were similar in character to those more terrible and extensive judgments which are to fall upon the world just before the *final deliverance* of God's people" (GC 627, 628).

He shows to His people that He is indeed the covenant-keeping God of Israel. This is the important principle which must guide us in the study of the 7 Trumpets and the 7 last Plagues. The almighty power of God exercised under the 7th plague is His answer to His people who are crying for deliverance from the death threatened by their enemies: "Yet to human sight it will appear that the people of God must soon seal their testimony with their blood as did the martyrs before them. They themselves begin to fear that the Lord has left them to fall by the hand of their enemies. It is a time of fearful agony. Day and night they cry unto God for *deliverance*" (GC 630). "Like the captive exile, they will be in fear of death by starvation or by violence. But the Holy One who divided *the Red Sea before Israel*, will manifest His mighty power and turn their captivity" (GC 634). The experiences at the Red Sea will be repeated. Then, "the Egyptians marched after them; and they were sore afraid: and the *children of Israel cried out unto the Lord*" (Ex. 14:10). The Lord answered their prayers, making a path through the deep—"the Lord made the sea dry land, and the waters were divided" (v. 21). The Egyptians who pursued them were destroyed: "The Lord overthrew the Egyptians in the midst of the sea . . . there remained not so much as one of them" (vs. 27, 28). Too late they discovered that they had been fighting God. They exclaimed: "Let us flee from the face of Israel; for the Lord fighteth for them against the Egyptians" (v. 25). This experience is to be repeated. Before spiritual Israel's enemies are destroyed "they find they have been fighting against God" (GC 640). "Even the enemies of our faith, persecutors, will perceive that God is working for His people in turning their captivity" (2SM 372). Their deliverance at the time of the 6th and 7th plagues (both of which commence the same night) and the destruction of their enemies during the 7th plague come in answer to their prayers—hence the linking up in the Scriptures of the 7 trumpets (God's judgments upon the persecutors of His people—in answer to their prayers) and the prayer Altar with the events under the 6th and the 7th plagues. From the principles already dealt with and those yet to be considered, we know that, of all the many passages throughout Holy Writ wherein the love of God for His people is revealed in delivering them from their enemies, none are more thrilling or more sanctifying than the Revelator's description of the 6th and 7th plagues. Nowhere is He more clearly revealed as the covenant-keeping God of Israel than in the study of the 6th and 7th plagues, a fact which the devil has striven so hard to hide.

The Euphrates is introduced in the Revelation in connection with the Prayer Altar (ch. 9:13, 14), and the significance of the drying up of the Euphrates (Rev. 16:12) cannot be discerned apart from the Prayer Altar. The Euphrates is "dried up" and God's people are delivered in answer to their prayers.

Some have suggested that the study of future events described in Holy Writ is not important because it is the *present* with which we have to do. It might be as logically reasoned that there is nothing to be gained by studying the *past* because it is the present that concerns us. However, it should be remembered that we are vitally helped in the present as we study the Word of God to discover how God helped His people in the past—"Whatsoever things were written aforetime *were written for* our learning, that we through patience and comfort of the Scriptures might have hope" (Rom. 15:4).

If our study of *future* events reveals the same as does our study of the past—the love of God for His people and the wise provisions He made for their care and protection—we will be helped even more. In fact, knowing that such loving and wise provisions are actually to be received or realized personally makes God's promises and assurances for the future more vital than even the comfort derived from the knowledge of how God had helped His people in the past. God has written much concerning the future in His Word because it does help us now. We become "partakers of the Divine nature" through the "exceeding great and precious promises" (2 Pet. 1:4). The promises concerning the Lord's return, of the resurrection, and the glories beyond, when believed and acted upon, do sanctify those who believe, for "every man that hath this hope in him purifieth himself, even as He is pure" (1 John 3:2, 3). The Lord completed His Word, giving His people a wonderful picture of the New Jerusalem, the capital of the eternal kingdom, because He knows that by contemplating upon the bliss to come believers will be stimulated in their effort to make sure that such endless joys will eventually be theirs. "And the Spirit and the bride say, Come" (Rev. 22:17). When Jesus said: "Sanctify them through Thy truth: Thy Word is truth" (John 17:17), He did not limit the sanctifying power of God's Word to that dealing with the present only. When the inspired Peter declared that the promises of God are among the agencies God has provided for partaking "of the Divine nature," that includes the promises that will be fulfilled in the future. "We must have a vision of the future and of the blessedness of heaven" (8T 44).

PRINCIPLE FIVE:
The Law of Growth or Development: the Principle of Repeat and Enlarge— the Repetition Contains an Explanation

A wise teacher takes his pupils so far, then, by a series of repetitions, goes from the known to the unknown. The Bible is based upon this wise principle. Later chapters or books develop the themes introduced earlier: "First the blade, then the ear, after that the full corn in the ear" (Mark 4:28). There is a remarkable parallel or similarity between Christian experience and nature, and the Scriptures. Plants grow from seed or bulb to the flower, fruit, or head. We are admonished to "*grow* in grace and in the knowledge of our Lord and Saviour, Jesus Christ." The Church is also to develop "unto a perfect man, unto the measure of the stature of the fullness of Christ . . . *grow up* into Him in all things, which is the Head" (Eph. 4:13-15). As all the nerves of the body lead to the brain, so do all the books of the Bible lead to the book of Revelation: "In the Revelation all the books of the Bible meet and end. Here is the complement of the book of Daniel. One is a prophecy; the other a revelation" (AA 585). Thus the book of Revelation throws light upon all the preceding books and must in itself be interpreted with remembrance of all the books that have preceded it. Some have not done this and have consequently misinterpreted some of its important prophecies. "The Word of God includes the Scriptures of the Old Testament as well as of the New. One is not complete without the other." "The Old Testament sheds light upon the New, and the New upon the Old" (COL 126, 128).

Simple illustrations of the principle of Repeat and Enlarge: Ex. 19:19 informs us that *"Moses spake"* as he beheld the terrifying splendours and heard the trumpet waxing louder and louder. We are not told what Moses said until Paul wrote. When Paul repeated the circumstances, he tells us *what* Moses spoke: "And so terrible was the sight, that *Moses said*, I exceedingly fear and quake" (Heb. 12:21).

Isaiah declared that when our Lord comes to awaken the sleeping saints He will use these words: "*Awake and sing*, ye that dwell in dust . . . and the earth shall cast out the dead" (Isa. 26:19). When Paul gave further details concerning the Second Advent and the resurrection, he said: "For the Lord Himself shall descend from heaven *with a shout* . . . and the dead in Christ shall rise first." Thus Paul informs us that our Lord will give "*a shout*," and Isaiah tells us *what* He will "shout": "*Awake and sing*, ye that dwell in dust." When Paul repeats instruction concerning this same event, he enlarges the picture by telling us *what* the righteous "*sing*" as they come from their dusty beds: "*Then* shall be brought to pass the saying that is written, Death is swallowed up in victory. O death, where is thy sting? O grave, where is thy victory?" (1 Cor. 15:54, 55).

All Bible doctrines are based upon this developmental plan, each repetition brings in additional features until in the Revelation the unfolding is completed: "The Word of God includes the Scriptures of the Old Testament as well as of the New. One is not complete without the other" (COL 126). Though Revelation completes the Word of God, it does not discard or render obsolete the Old Testament, but is complementary, supplementary, explanatory. "The student should learn to view the Word as a whole, and to see *the relation of its parts*" (Ed 190; CT 462).

God chose the Hebrew nation and language as His channels of communication. An obvious characteristic of expression shown in the Old Testament is that of "Parallelisms," or the repetition of thought which contains an explanation of what has been stated. Words or phrases of substantially the same import occurring in parallel or antithetical clauses are repeated in an explanatory, or expansive way: "In the way of righteousness is *life*; and in the pathway thereof there is *no death*" (Prov. 12:28). "He shall bring forth thy righteousness as the *light*, and thy judgment as the *noonday*"—at noon the light of day is at its maximum strength, so the "light" at first mentioned is enlarged upon in the repetition. Another simple illustration is found in Isa. 1:16 where the same thought is presented with four variations, but with each repetition the message becomes more emphatic and clearer in its meaning. The Old Testament abounds with these "Parallelisms," of repeating and enlarging upon what has been said.

Application:

The books of Daniel and Revelation are based upon this principle of repeating and enlarging, which assists us in comprehending its prophecies.

From Matt. 7:2, 7 we observe that our Lord employed this principle. As He is "The Revelator" (Rev. 22:16; GC 342), we are not surprised that the Apocalypse, also, is based upon the principle of repeat and enlarge. The Lord's servant says that the Revelation deals with "the *same* subjects" as does Daniel, that "the book of Daniel is unsealed in the Revelation to John," that "the things revealed to Daniel were afterwards *complemented* by the Revelation," which gives "*further* light on the subjects dealt with in Daniel" (TM 114-118). "The books of Daniel and Revelation are one. One is a prophecy, the other a revelation; one a book sealed, the other a book opened" (Ms 59, 1900). That is, the Revelation is the Lord's explanation of Daniel, and of all books preceding it. The light is clearer or more complete in Revelation. This is in harmony with the principle operating throughout the Word of God of repeating what has already been mentioned, but repeating in order to explain more fully.

This same principle is clearly revealed in the book of Daniel, for the vision of Dan. 2 is repeated and enlarged upon in chapter 7, and again repeated and enlarged upon in Dan. 8, 9. Daniel's last prophecy was given him in answer to his request for light on the prophecy concerning the 2300 days, the cleansing of the sanctuary, and the experiences of God's people until the close of the great controversy; events which had been previously mentioned in Daniel. This principle enables us to see that Turkey could not possibly be the king of the north, for the explanation deals only with what has already been mentioned, and Turkey has not been mentioned in the earlier prophecies of Daniel. The repetitions enlarge upon something already mentioned. The vision of Dan. 2 depicts ancient Babylon and the events that lead to spiritual Babylon, which will seek to unite the broken fragments of the Roman Empire through spiritual ties. "The mingling of church craft and state craft is represented by the iron and the clay" (Ms 63, 1899). [1] In this application of the prophecy of Dan. 2, the Lord's servant reveals that this prophecy outlines the final phases of the great controversy between Christ and Satan. Consequently, every prophecy in Daniel enlarges upon this theme. As so much space is occupied with the king of the north it could not be anything else than an enlargement of preceding prophecies given to explain about literal Babylon and the course of history leading to last-day spiritual Babylon. As "the things revealed to Daniel were afterward *complemented* by the revelation made to John," and "both [books] relate to the *same* subjects" (TM 114, 117) we know that the drying up of the Euphrates could not possibly refer to Turkey, but could mean only the ending of Babylon, the king of the north (Ezek. 26:7; 25:9; 46:6, 10, etc.).

The theme of the first prophecy of the Bible (Gen. 3:15—the conflict between the dragon and her seed) is repeated and enlarged upon in the final conflict (Rev. 12:17). Chapters 12 to 20 of Revelation present the events leading to the final conflict and describe the whole world involved in this terrible struggle. Those who follow Bible principles of interpretation—the repetition and enlargement of the same thing—will have no difficulty in understanding the Revelator's graphic portrayal as he describes the *"war"* in heaven (Rev. 12:7). He traces that same war (Rev. 13:4, 7; 16:14; 17:14; 19:11, 19; 20:8) down to earth, to Eden and then on to its final stage (Rev. 16:12-21) when all the powers of earth will be brought into conflict with God's Government by commanding His subjects to refuse to obey His Sabbath command. Rev. 17 *repeats* the revelation contained in Rev. 16, and gives further details of how Babylon is restored to her power of persecution and sits upon the "many waters" of the Euphrates (Rev. 17:1, 15). Further details are also given as to what is meant by the drying up of the waters of the Euphrates (v. 16, 17)—the people thus symbolized destroy their spiritual guardians who have led them to persecute God's people—"their evil work will recoil upon themselves" (Ms 63, 1899). Rev. 18 repeats and enlarges upon the destruction that

1 See 4BC 1168, 1169 for the full statement of Ms 63, 1899

comes to Babylon, and Rev. 19 repeats and enlarges upon the destruction which is completed by the Saviour's Second Coming. The same principle operates in Christian experience and in the construction of the Scriptures—the light "shineth *more and more* unto the perfect day" (Prov. 4:18).

WHO ARE "THE KINGS FROM THE SUNRISING" (Rev. 16:12)?

By this principle of repeating and enlarging, which may be discerned throughout the Apocalypse, we know that "the kings from the sunrising" of Rev. 16:12 could not possibly refer to nations to the "East" of Palestine, because if they were *they would be referred to again in later passages.* However, when "the kings from the sunrising" are interpreted to describe "the armies of heaven" coming to deliver the Israel of God from this Babylonian world, we see the application of this principle of *repeat and enlarge* in the fact that these "armies of heaven" are more fully described in Rev. 19:11-21. In the extracts already presented (pp. 8, 9), the Lord's servant has given us the key for arriving at the truth of such problems: "The Word of God, as a whole, is a perfect chain, one portion *linking into and explaining another*" (EW 221). "The Bible is its own interpreter, *one passage explaining another*" (4T 499). "Every prophecy *an explanation of another*" (Ed 123). The principle clearly revealed throughout Scripture is that explanations are presented in the repetitions. The "war" of Rev. 16:12-16 is again referred to and explained more fully in Rev. 17:12-17 and again in Rev. 19:11-21. Our *Commentary* says: "Proponents of both views agree that different aspects *of the same battle* are described in chapters. 14:14-20; 16:12-19; 17:14-17; 19:11-21" (7BC 845).

No important Bible teaching stands on one verse. If "the kings of the east" referred to the nations to the East of Palestine that would make them more important than all the others in the prophecy, for they would be mentioned *twice* in the same picture: (1) "the kings of the East"; (2) and also *included* in the words: "the kings of the earth and the whole world." Thus, in contrast, the Papal-Protestant "West" would be mentioned only once in Rev. 16:12-16 though looming so large throughout chapters 12-19. The incongruity of the interpretation, which makes the kings of the east refer to nations to the East of Palestine, becomes more obvious when observing that, in the repetitions and enlargements (Rev. 17:12-17; 19:11-21) of the war of Rev. 16:12-16, no mention is made at all of these Eastern nations, *as would be the case* were they the kings of the east mentioned in Rev. 16:12. The erroneous interpretation presents an illogical balance, which may be stated briefly: Eastern nations twice in Rev. 16:12-16 but not again; the Protestant-Papal powers in a lesser role because mentioned only once in Rev. 16:12-16. However, the truth is that the beast and the false prophet are *religious* powers leading out in a *religious* war against God's people—they lead the whole world in this war. This in itself shows that the kings of the east cannot refer to earthly powers or they, too, would be led by the powers of Christendom in this war—instead of being interpreted as being more important by being mentioned twice. In succeeding visions the beast and the false prophet—religious powers—are the leaders in the war against Christ and His people, and in these later descriptions of this war no special mention is made of the Eastern nations. In other words, the powers of Christendom are pictured in each vision of the war, as leading out and bringing all nations on to the side of Satan. Thus the kings of the east could not refer to earthly powers which are firstly, given special mention and, secondly, included with the kings of the earth and the whole world. The fact that later visions of this war present the powers of Christendom as the dominant leaders shows that they are the dominant leaders in the vision of Rev. 16:12-16. Our analysis of 16:12-16 that the kings of the east cannot refer to earthly powers is corroborated by the fact that they are not described as such in the later, explanatory prophecies.

A number of commentators have pointed out that "the kings of the east" are mentioned as a separate class from, and at war with, "the kings of the earth and the whole world": "The kings of the earth who are earthly (v. 14) *stand in contrast to the kings from the East, who are heavenly*" (*Commentary by Jamieson, Faussett and Brown*). "The 'Kings of the East' are *certainly ranged on the side of God*. Many writers see an allusion to Christ and His saints. The sun is a frequent figure of Christ in the Scriptures (cf. Mal. 4:2; Zech. 3:8; 6:12; LXX, Luke 1:78; also Rev. 7:2; 12:1; 22:16). *The Kings of the East may thus be identified with the armies of Rev. 19:11-16*" (*The Pulpit Commentary*). In his, *The Book of*

Revelation, p. 269, W. Milligan, D.D., comments on Rev. 16:12-16:—"We have also met at Rev. 7:2 with the expression 'from the sunrising,' and it is there applied to the quarter from which the angel comes by whom the people of God are sealed. In a book so carefully written as the Apocalypse, it is not easy to think of anti-Christian foes coming from a quarter described in the same terms. *These kings from the sunrising are not said to be part of* 'the kings of the whole inhabited earth' immediately afterwards referred to. *They are rather distinguished from them.* . . . The type of drying up the waters of a river takes us back, alike in the historical and prophetic writings of the Old Testament, to the means by which the Almighty secures the deliverance of His people."

That the kings of the east refer to the armies of heaven may be discerned by heeding the principle revealed throughout the Scriptures—the principle of repeating and enlarging and explaining what is introduced earlier. That the "war" (RV) of Rev. 16:12-16 is the same war as the "war" of Rev. 19:11-21 may be seen readily by comparing the terminology in both descriptions and by observing statements from the Spirit of Prophecy—GC 640, 641; 6T 406—commenting upon Rev. 19:11-21. Note the following summary:

Rev. 16:21	Rev. 19:11-21
v. 12: "And I saw,"	v. 11: "And I saw"
"The kings of the east"	"Soon there appears in the east"
	"Jesus rides forth a mighty Conqueror"
	"The King of kings, and Lord of Lords"
	"The armies of heaven . . . follow Him"
v. 16: "God Almighty"	v. 15: "Almighty God"
"Armageddon"	"Armageddon" (6T 406; GC 640, 641)
v. 13: "beast,"	v. 19, 20: "beast,"
"false prophet"	

v. 14: "miracles"

v. 14, 16: "gathered"

v. 14: "to the war" (RV)

v. 14: "The *Ruler* of all" (*Weymouth*) "The *sovereign* Lord" (NEB)

TM 465: "An alliance with Satan against heaven, and join in battle against the *Ruler* of the universe:"

GC 624: "Against the *government* of heaven."

v. 20: "miracles"

v. 19: "gathered"

v. 19: "to make war against" Christ

v. 20: "the mark of the beast": is opposed to the sign of "the *authority* of God" (8T 118; TM 134).

As "different aspects of the same battle are described in chs. 14:14-20; 16:12-19; 17:14-17; 19:11-21" (7BC 845), and not the slightest mention, specifically, is made of the nations to the East of Palestine in the repetitions and explanations—Rev. 17:14-17; 19:11-21—of the "war" described in 16:12-16, we know for certain that they are not singled out in 16:12-16 for any special emphasis. However, as "the armies of heaven" are mentioned in the explanatory repetition we know that they are the kings of the east referred to in Rev. 16:12.

PRINCIPLE SIX:
The Law of the World-wide Symbolized by the Local

All the prophets employed the principle of the world-wide symbolized by the local. "His [Zephaniah's] prophecies of impending judgment upon Judah apply with equal force to the judgments that are to fall upon an impenitent *world* at the time of the second advent of Christ" (PK 389). "Christ saw in Jerusalem a symbol of the *world* . . . hastening on to meet the retributive judgments of God." "The Saviour's prophecy concerning the visitation of judgments upon Jerusalem is to have another fulfillment . . . the doom of a *world*" (GC 22, 36).

Numerous examples could be cited of the use of the local which is employed as a symbol of worldwide occurrences at the end of time—this principle runs throughout the Bible. As stated by Dr. Angus: "From the *typical* character of ancient dispensations arises another peculiarity of prophecy. It not only *speaks their language*, but it has often a *double* application. It applies to one object by anticipation and partially, and to another completely; the earlier object being the *representative* of the later. . . . It follows from this *double* sense that, as in the first fulfillment there is a limit to the blessing foretold, so, in the second, there is a fullness of meaning which it seems impossible to exhaust" (*Bible Handbook*, pp. 285-292).

Application:

Throughout this presentation this principle is illustrated. It is revealed in so many places of Scripture that it is generally recognized. Prophecies concerning Assyria and Babylon end with the statement: "This is the purpose that is purposed upon the *whole world*" (Isa. 14:22-26). Prophecies given by Isaiah,

Jeremiah, Ezekiel, and other of the prophets, have a double application—one, to be fulfilled locally; the other, to be fulfilled on a worldwide scale in the last days. God's last-day Message is based upon this principle. At the commencement of the 2300 days prophecy, literal Israel was called out of literal Babylon "to restore and to build Jerusalem" (Dan. 9:25), to rebuild the temple the Babylonians had destroyed. At the ending of the 2300 days prophecy, spiritual Israel is being called out of spiritual Babylon (Rev. 18:4) "to restore all things" (Matt. 17:11; Rev. 14:6-14, etc.); to rebuild the spiritual temple (Rev. 11:1; GC 266), and repair the walls of the church (Is. 58:12-14, etc.), which spiritual Babylon had spoiled (PK 677, 678).

Jezebel led Israel to substitute pagan principles of worship for the true worship of God: the Revelator employs her as a symbol of the Papacy (Rev. 2:20). Jezebel, aided by Ahab at the head of the State, fostered sun-worship among Israel. The Papacy aided by the State, fosters Sun-day observance among professing Christians. Then, a false priesthood was instituted (1 Kings 16:32, 33; 18:22-40). In the Christian era a false priesthood has been instituted (1 Tim. 2:5). Then, they ignored God's commandments (1 Kings 18:18). The Papacy has thought itself able to change God's Law (Dan. 7:25). Then, there were 3 1/2 *literal* years drought (1 Kings 17:1; 18:1; Jas. 5:17, 18). There were 3 1/2 *symbolic* years of *spiritual* drought in the Christian era (Dan. 7:25; 12:7; Rev. 12:6, 14; 13:5). Jezebel was "thrown to the dust" (2 Kings 9:30, 33). The spiritual Jezebel will be thrown to the dust (Rev. 18:7, 8, etc.). Elijah's work was to restore the true worship of God (1 Kings 18:18-39). The anti-typical Elijah Message restores the true worship of God (Mal. 4:4, 5; Rev. 7:1-4; 14:6-12). Elijah was translated to heaven without dying (2 Kings 2:11). People who proclaim the worldwide Elijah message, who live until the coming of Christ, will be translated to heaven without seeing death (Rev. 14:3, 6-14). The prophets of Baal were brought from the mountain "down to the brook Kishon" where they were all slain (1 Kings 18:40). In Judges 5:19-23 "the river Kishon" is identified as "the waters of *Megiddo*." Modern prophets of Baal worship will be destroyed in the anti-typical, worldwide slaughter of Armageddon. Many such applications could be cited from the Old Testament—the local being employed as a type of worldwide events in the last days.

The judgments upon Jerusalem foreshadowed "the doom of the world" (GC 22, 37). Before the judgments fell upon Jerusalem a message of warning was sounded, rejected (GC 23), and probation closed (Luke 19:41-44; Matt. 23:38; GC 21). Before judgments fall upon the world a message of warning is being sounded and it will, in the main, be rejected (GC 37), and probation will close (Rev. 22:11; GC 38, 491). The last sign given before the judgments fell upon Jerusalem was that of the Roman armies gathered outside the city walls (Matt. 24:15; Luke 21:20; 5T 451, 464; GC 26, 37, 38). The last sign before the 7 last plagues fall upon the world will be the Roman armies—the world powers under the influence of the Papacy—poised to destroy spiritual Israel for refusing the mark of the beast (5T, 451; 464). This was the sign to the early believers to flee from Jerusalem to the mountains (GC 26, 38, 31). This will be the sign to God's remnant people to take their flight to the mountains (5T 464; GC 38).

As the things of Israel are employed as types of *worldwide* events in the experiences of the church and her enemies, the application of the locality of Israel (Rev. 16:12-16; Dan. 11:45, etc.)—Megiddo, Jerusalem, the Euphrates—in relation to anything of a literal, local, Palestinian character is shown to be out of harmony with the principles of interpretation shown throughout the Bible.

PRINCIPLE SEVEN:
The Law of the Significance
of Bible Names:

A decided connection exists between the proper names of the Bible and its history and doctrines. The Hebrews attached great importance to the meaning of proper names—the meaning determined the name—a fact which must be remembered when studying the Scriptures, for often there is a deliberate play upon the meaning of a word. Dr. Angus states: "Nearly all the names in Hebrew are significant, and a knowledge of their meaning throws a light upon its context" (*Bible Handbook*, p. 185).

"Adam called his wife's name Eve [margin, *Living*]; *because* she was the mother of all *living*" (Gen. 3:20). "Thou shalt call His name Jesus (margin, *Saviour*): *for* He shall *save* His people from their sins" (Matt. 1:21). Sometimes important aspects of prophetical understanding depend upon the meaning of a name. For instance, in the interpretation of the 2300 days, or years, of Dan. 8:14; 9:24-27, we need to know the meaning of the word "*Messiah*," for the prophecy—"unto the *Messiah*"—brings us to A.D. 27. Jesus was not born in A.D. 27. The key is in the *meaning* of the word Messiah, which is given in John 1:41, margin: "We have found the Messias, which is, being interpreted, *the Christ, or the Anointed*." At His birth, Our Lord was given the name of "Jesus," but He did not become "Christ"—"the Messiah," or "the Anointed"—until the time of His baptism in A.D. 27 (Luke 3:21-23; 4:1, 14-16; Acts 10:38). It was then that Jesus, referring to Daniel's prophecy, proclaimed: "the time is fulfilled" (Mark 1:9-11). Daniel prophesied that "the Messiah," "the Anointed," "the Christ," would commence His work of confirming the New Covenant (Dan. 9:27), which, as also prophesied in Dan. 9:27, He ratified by the shedding of His blood 3 $^1/_2$ years later. The true interpretation of this prophecy, also the proof that Jesus fulfilled it, depends upon the meaning of the word "Messiah."

The meanings of the Names of the prophets were frequently keys to their books.

"Daniel" means "God is judge." His book describes (1) the judgment upon Babylon (Dan. 5:26-28). (2) The Judgment in the heavenly sanctuary (Dan. 7:9, 10). (3) The time prophecy concerning the hour of God's investigative Judgment (8:14; 9:24-26; Rev. 14:6, 7). (4) The close of the investigative Judgment (Dan. 12:1).

"Jeremiah" means "whom Jehovah launched forth." The references to him being sent of God are a play upon the meaning of His name (Jer. 1:17; 19:1-3; 22:1, 2, etc.). "Micah" means "Who is like unto the Lord." Micah 7:18 is a play upon the meaning of the name "Micah." Very often God commanded a name to be given. The meaning of Isaac's name suggests *joyous laughter*, and God told Abraham to name his child Isaac. When promised a child, "Abraham . . . *laughed*. . . . And God said . . . thou shalt call his name Isaac" (Gen. 17:17-19). In Gen. 18 we see the play upon the meaning of "*Isaac*." When the Lord (with Abraham outside his tent) repeated the promise of the child, Sarah, inside the tent, heard it and "*laughed* within herself. . . . And the Lord said unto Abraham, Wherefore did Sarah laugh?. . . Then Sarah denied, saying, I *laughed* not; for she was afraid. And He said, Nay; but thou didst *laugh*" (Gen. 18:9-15). When Isaac was born, "Sarah said, God hath made me to *laugh*, so that all that hear will *laugh with me*" (Gen. 21:3, 6). Paul points out that Isaac is a type of Christians: "Now we, brethren, as Isaac was, are the children of promise" (Gal. 4:28). Isaac's name suggests joyous laughter, and *joy* is the second fruit of the Spirit (Gal. 5:22). Isaac's name suggests joy now, and also points to the joy of the saved: "In Thy presence is *fullness of joy*; at Thy right hand there are pleasures for evermore" (Ps. 16:11).

"Isaiah" means "the salvation of the Lord." The term salvation is more frequently used in his book than in other prophetic books; he is known as "the gospel prophet." His child's name was given by God as a message to the people—see Isa. 8:1-4, 18. God selected the names of some other prophets because their meanings carried messages for His professed people then, and also for subsequent years. God gave Solomon his name (1 Chron. 22:9, 10) because of the play upon the meaning of his name.

Because Esau was born "*red . . .* they called his name *Esau,*" and because the second twin "*took hold* on Esau's heel, his name was called *Jacob*" (Gen. 25:25, 26). In Gen. 27:36, margin, we see how Esau made a play upon the meaning of "Jacob": "And he [Esau] said, Is not he rightly named Jacob, that is, the *Supplanter*? for he hath *supplanted* me these two times: he *took away* my birthright and, behold, now he hath *taken away* my blessing." When Jacob's character was changed God changed his name: "Thy name shall be called no more Jacob, but *Israel, that is, a prince of God*: for as a *prince* hast thou power with God and with men, and hast *prevailed*" (Gen. 32:27, 28, margin). The name "*Israel*" in the New Testament stands for those who, like Jacob, have wrestled with God in prayer until their characters have become changed into the divine similitude. Israelites are a praying people. This is shown in Nathanael's experience: "Jesus saw Nathanael coming to Him, and saith of him, Behold an *Israelite indeed,* in whom is no guile," because Nathanael had spent time with God in prayer in the secrecy of an overhanging fig tree. Jesus' all-seeing eye had seen what others did not see. It was enough! Nathanael then knew that Jesus was the promised Messiah, and so proclaimed: "Thou art the *King of Israel*" (John 1:47-50).

The principle of playing upon the meaning of names runs throughout the Bible.

Application:

The application of the law of the meaning of names is imperative to the understanding of the prophecies of the last days. The meaning of the name helps clarify the prophecy. "Malachi" means "Messenger of the Lord." In Mal. 3:1 we read: "I will send my *messenger . . .* the *messenger* of the covenant." This book, written for those professing to be God's messengers, closes (4:5, 6) with the prophecy of the coming of Elijah. The partial (Palestinian) fulfillment in the experience of John the Baptist (Matt. 17:11-13; Luke 1:13-17; John 1:19-23) revealed that the emphasis would be upon the *message* proclaimed. Combining the law that the local of the Old Testament becomes the worldwide in the New, we know that the last-day application of this prophecy is not for the coming of Elijah in person, but the coming of a worldwide *message* warning the world of the coming of the judgments of God.

The meaning of Abraham's name helps us understand Rev. 7:9. The Spirit of Prophecy applies the "great multitude" of Rev. 7:9 to the redeemed of all ages (1T 79, 155; *The Spirit of Prophecy,* vol. 3, p. 253; GC 665). The Lord gave His reason for changing Abram's name: "Neither shall thy name any more be called Abram, but thy name shall be Abraham; for a *father of many nations* have I made thee" (Gen. 17:4, 5). The New Testament often makes a play upon the meaning of Abraham's name, calling him "the *father* of all them that believe" (Rom. 4:11-18; Gal. 3:7-29; Rev. 21:24). The "great multitude" of the saved (Rev. 7:9), are the spiritual children of Abraham "the *father* of a great multitude."

The meanings of the names of "Edom" or "Esau" and "Bozrah" help us to understand "Armageddon," meaning "Mount of Slaughter." The prophecy of Isa. 34 depicts a great slaughter, which expositors generally agree is the coming Armageddon. *The Scripture Gazetteer,* p. 330, in its comments on Isa. 34, says: "The original sense of these words aptly applies to a place of slaughter. *Edom*, signifying *red as blood*, and *Bozrah, a vintage,* which, in prophetic language, often denotes God's vengeance upon the wicked." Jesus selected wine as a symbol of His blood (Matt. 26:27-29). Roman Catholics teach that when Jesus said, "This is My body . . . this is My blood," He intended us to take His words *literally*, and not symbolically. Jesus did not need to state that the bread and wine were *symbols*, for in the Old Testament these were employed symbolically. The names of Edom, Idumea and Bozrah are employed in Isa. 34 and 63 because of their symbolical meanings. Such prophecies as Isa. 63:1-6; Jer. 25:30-33; Joel 3:13, 14; Rev. 14:14-20, can be fully understood only when the meanings of these names are applied, especially in their last-day worldwide application to the "Mount of Slaughter"—"Armageddon."

Jacob feared that he would be slain by his brother Esau. The experience of Jacob (who overcame through prayer) with Esau, or Edom ('red as blood'), has its worldwide application in the last days: "Jacob's night of anguish, when he wrestled in prayer for deliverance from the hand of Esau (Gen. 32:24-30), represents the experience of God's people in the time of trouble. . . . As Satan influenced Esau to march against Jacob, so he will stir up the wicked to destroy God's people in the time of trouble" (GC 616-618). Thus God's servant refers to Esau as a *type* of those who will endeavour to slay God's people in the last days; thus showing the principle by which Isa. 34 and 63 should be interpreted. Edom, Idumea, and Bozrah are no more to be literally understood than Esau or Jacob or Israel. Esau and his descendants are mentioned in Scriptures as having hatred against Israel (Gen. 27:41; Obadiah 10, etc.). The Revelator draws his imagery of the destruction of all the wicked from Isa. 34: compare v. 4 with Rev. 6:13, 14; v. 10 with Rev. 14:11, 18; 18:18; 19:3, etc. Thus their slaughter, said to occur in Edom or Bozrah, actually symbolizes the destruction of all the enemies of spiritual Israel in the "mount of slaughter"—"Armageddon."

The names of places mentioned in the prophecies of the book of Revelation are intended to be symbolical: "The names of the seven churches are *symbolic* of the church in different periods of the Christian Era" (AA 585). Rev. 1:1 says that signs or symbols are employed in the book. Consequently, it was not necessary to say that these first 7 places were symbols. That principle operates in the Revelation until the coming of Christ renders symbols obsolete. As the things of Israel are applied earlier in the New Testament as belonging to the church, it was unnecessary to state in the Revelation that the Jewish things therein were to be applied to the church. The very fact that John wrote that the world is gathered "into a place called in the *Hebrew* tongue Armageddon" (Rev. 16:16) is sufficient to make it plain that the word was intended to be a *symbol* and that the key lay in understanding the *meaning* of the word in the *Hebrew* tongue. In John 5:2 the apostle drew attention to the name of the pool where Jesus manifested His pity and mercy upon a man who had brought disease upon himself through sin. Jesus *pitied* him, bending in compassion over him, saying "Wilt thou be made whole?" and He had *mercy* upon him and forgave him, saying: "Sin no more, lest a worse thing come unto thee" (vs. 6, 14). In introducing this touching and significant miracle the gospel evangelist, frequently making spiritual applications, drew attention to the *name* of the pool "in the *Hebrew* tongue Bethesda"—meaning "House of Pity or Mercy." The meaning of that name expressed the spiritual lesson he endeavoured to convey to his readers. Similarly in Rev. 16:16.

The Hebrew emphasis runs throughout the Apocalypse: "The writer does, then, *intentionally Hebraise*. . . . Nothing can be more decided than his [Ewald's] statement that the imitation of Hebrew idiom in the Apocalypse goes so far as to lead to many a change in Greek construction with the view of imitating the construction of the Hebrew tongue" (Dr. W. Milligan, *The Revelation of St. John*, p. 260).

In Rev. 9:11 John directs us to "the *Hebrew* tongue" to convey his meaning.

Uriah Smith (*Daniel and the Revelation*, p. 479), in commenting upon Rev. 9:11, says: "His name. In Hebrew, 'Abaddon,' the destroyer; in Greek, 'Apollyon,' one that exterminates, or destroys. Having two different names in two languages, it is evident that the *character*, rather than the name of the power, is intended to be represented . . . as expressed in both languages he is a destroyer." As the *character* of the power and not its *literal* name is expressed in the Hebrew name of Rev. 9:11, so it is because of the *character* or the *meaning* "in the *Hebrew* tongue" of the word Armageddon that it is mentioned in Rev. 16:16. We are directed to the *Hebrew* to emphasize again that this slaughter pertains to the enemies of the *church*, "the Israel of God" (Gal. 6:16), and as the anti-type of the things of Israel is shown in the New Testament to be *worldwide*, a worldwide conflict *against the church* is pictured in the prophecy of Rev. 16:12-16.

The Importance of the Meaning of Bible Names—

Our Lord Jesus gave names because of their meanings.

In Mark 3: 16 we read: "And Simon He surnamed Peter; and James . . . John the brother of James; and *He surnamed them Boanerges*, which is, *The sons of thunder*." He gave Simon a name which expressed his character: "And when Jesus beheld him, He said, Thou art Simon the son of Jona: thou shalt be called Cephas, which is by interpretation, A *stone*, margin, or, *Peter*" (John 1:42). Peter, the movable "*stone*" is not the foundation of the church. Jesus, Whom Peter acknowledged to be "the

Christ, the Son of the living God" (Matt. 16:16)—He Who is known throughout the Old Testament as "the *Rock* of Israel" (2 Sam. 23:3; 22:2, 32; Deut. 32:4, 15, 18; Isa. 17:10; Ps. 18:2, etc.) is the immovable "*Rock*" upon Whom the church is built (Matt. 16:18; Eph. 2:20; 1 Pet. 2:5-8; 1 Cor. 10:4; Matt. 7:24, 25). The importance of observing the play upon the meaning of Bible names is made manifest in that millions of Roman Catholics are palpably deceived by Papal assumptions based upon a failure to heed this important principle, as shown in the Lord making a contrasting play upon the meaning of the name "Peter" and the immovable *Rock* upon which He builds His church. Similarly, millions of Protestants have been deceived concerning the meaning of the "Armageddon" prophecy because they, too, have failed to heed the way the Lord Jesus, the Revelator, has made a play upon the meaning of that word in "the Hebrew tongue" in Rev. 16:16.

PRINCIPLE EIGHT:
The Law Governing "Spiritual" Interpretations:

God is the Author of "spiritual" interpretations. It is a mistake to think that "spiritual" interpretations take one into an unreal world, a world of fancy, conjecture, imagination, for they take one into a world of actuality—they are mental pictures—imagery—of spiritual truths which are *based upon things that have actually happened*. It is God's principle of preaching per pictures, "similitudes" (Hosea 12:10), "acted parables."

A "similitude" is an "image" or "likeness" (Jas. 3:9 compare with Gen. 1:26, 27). God employed likenesses, or *imagery* because He created the mind capable of conjuring up pictures. Educationalists rightly stress the value of "visual education." The blessings of eyesight are very great; but the blessings of *mind-sight* are greater. Clear thinking is an alert mind taking clear pictures, which are stored up in the memory. We forget easily when we fail to expose the mind-plate long enough to enable the picture to be indelibly stamped upon the mind. Meditation is a Christian duty (1 Tim. 4:15). Reading the Bible daily makes Scriptural pictures more permanent. By word-pictures God has made the truths of His Word clear, and by them He has been able to present "much in little." The picture of an innocent, unblemished lamb, slain because of an individual's sin, presents an impressive picture of Christ's substitutionary death. Who is so blind as not to be powerfully impressed by the word-picture of the Israelites sheltering behind the blood-sprinkled door lintels while the death angel passes by, thus illustrating the effectiveness of the blood of Jesus to save. David's victorious conflict with the great Goliath provides us with a clear picture of what it means to live the victorious life in the power of Christ. The historical incidents recorded in the Old Testament provide us with word pictures by which God teaches us spiritual truths. In them we see things *worldwide* in scope—they are "spiritually discerned" (1 Cor. 2:6-16).

In the days of Jeremiah, "the Lord taught the people by means of a series of *acted parables*" (PK 423). "Acted parables" presented pictures of spiritual things. When on earth Jesus pointed to nature in teaching spiritual truths: word-pictures of earthly things with heavenly meanings: "The unknown was *illustrated by the known*; divine truths by earthly things with which the people were most familiar. The Scripture says, 'All these things spake Jesus unto the multitude in parables'. . . . Natural things were the medium for the spiritual; the things of nature . . . were connected with the truths of the written Word. Leading thus from the natural to the spiritual kingdom. . . . *No more effective method of instruction could He have employed*" (COL 17-21). "A wise purpose underlay every act of Christ's life on earth" (DA 206). He taught spiritual lessons in every miracle performed (DA 266, 267, 336, 341, etc.). "The cursing of the fig tree was *an acted parable*. . . . He invested the tree with moral qualities, and made it *the expositor of divine truth*" (DA 582). "Every act of His life, every word spoken, every miracle wrought, was to make known to fallen humanity the infinite love of God" (PK 696).

The New Testament fully enunciates the principle that the *literal* things which were enacted in Palestine were "acted parables"—presenting pictures, or types, of *worldwide, spiritual* things pertaining to Christ's spiritual kingdom of grace.

Application:

The Lord emphasized the value of "spiritual" interpretations when He had the experiences of His people recorded in the Old Testament to be spiritually applied by His church: "For whatsoever things were written aforetime *were written* for our learning, that we through patience and comfort of the Scriptures might have hope" (Rom. 15:4). Not only were these things written, but Paul declared that they *"were written for our learning."* Thus it is clearly stated that God had these things recorded to be employed for His people in New Testament times: this includes *"whatsoever* things were written"—which covers far more than the sanctuary and its meaningful services. Again Paul states:

"Now *all* these things happened unto them for types [margin]: and they are written *for* our admonition, upon whom the ends of the world are come" (1 Cor. 10:11). In this instance, also, Paul does not limit the use of types and antitypes to the sanctuary and its services. He refers to the experiences of Israel, the historical incidents recorded in the Old Testament. Again Paul stresses the fact that God purposefully had "*all*" those experiences "written *for* our admonition" in the Old Testament as types of the experiences of His people living in New Testament times. In this very passage Paul quotes a few of the experiences and shows what he means: "And did all eat the same *spiritual* meat; and did all drink the same *spiritual* drink: for they drank of that *spiritual* Rock that went with them: and that Rock was Christ" (vs. 3, 4 margin). The literal manna, the literal water, and the literal rock, have "*spiritual*" counterparts in the kingdom of Christ—He is the Manna that sustained His people in their wilderness journey. The smitten rock points to the Cross of Jesus, from whence flowed "the water of life" which satisfies all His pilgrim people.

The "spiritual" application of the things of Israel runs all through the New Testament. Without understanding the principles which govern their antitypical use, one cannot discern the real significance of certain prophecies in the book of Revelation. Jesus applied the giving of manna as the giving of Himself—the living Bread—(John 6). "Like the manna given in the wilderness, His grace is bestowed daily, for the day's need. Like the hosts of Israel in their pilgrim life, we may find morning by morning the bread of heaven for the day's supply" (MB 101).

The rejected stone, which later became "the head of the corner" (Ps. 118:22), Jesus applied to Himself (Matt. 21:42). Peter, also, applied it thus, and then "*spiritually*" applied the temple, the priesthood, and the sacrifices: "Ye also, as lively stones, are built up a *spiritual* house, an holy priesthood, to offer up *spiritual* sacrifices, acceptable to God" (1 Pet. 2:5). The ancient temple was built silently (1 Kings 6:7), and this is typical of the silent working of the Holy Spirit in building the spiritual temple (Eph. 2:21, 22). The following few examples, stated very briefly, illustrate the way the New Testament applies the "things" of Israel in a "*spiritual*" sense in connection with Christ's "mysterious *spiritual* kingdom of which He spoke" (DA 391).

Old Testament History	The New Testament Spiritual Application.
"The first Adam"—father of a sinful, mortal race.	1 Cor. 15:45-49. Jesus, "the last Adam", the Father of a sinless, immortal race.
Eve—Adam's wife.	Eph. 5:31, 32; Gen. 2:23, 24. The Church—the bride of "the last Adam."
Melchisedec, the king-priest of Salem.	Heb. 7:2-6. Typified Jesus, "The King of Righteousness," the "King of Peace," Who reigns in "the Heavenly Jerusalem" (12:22).
Abraham, the father of the tribes of Israel.	Rom. 4:11-18. "The father of all them that believe," Rom. 9:7, 8; Gal. 3:7-9, etc.
Isaac, the promised seed.	Matt. 1:1; Gal. 3:16; 4:28. Type of Jesus; also type of those who are Christ's.
Isaac, miraculously born of a freewoman, was free.	Gal. 4:28. Type of Christians who are born again of the Holy Spirit.
Israelites.	Rom. 2:28, 29; 9:7, 8; Gal. 3:29; Rev. 7:4-8; 21:12-14, etc. Christians.

To write out all the spiritual applications made in the New Testament of the things of Israel would fill a book, for this principle enters into the warp and the woof of its design.

One general law governs the employment of these spiritual applications—they are applied thus in connection with Christ's *"spiritual* kingdom," which is *worldwide in scope.* In Gen. 12:7; 13:14, Abraham and his seed were promised Palestine; in Rom. 4:13, Paul says that Abraham and his seed were promised *"the world."*

Not only did Israel's sanctuary and services foreshadow greater things to come, but the liberation from Egypt, the experiences at the Red Sea, the desert experiences, their entrance into the promised land, etc., were written as "types," "figures," or "acted parables," illustrating the experiences of the *worldwide* church and her enemies.

It will be noted that the *"spiritual"* applications brought to view in the New Testament are based upon things that actually occurred—the literal is the commencement of, or the foundation for, the spiritual. God leads our minds from the material world to the spiritual. "That was not first which is spiritual, but that which is natural; and afterward that which is spiritual" (1 Cor. 15:46). God employs the material world to teach spiritual lessons.

The book of Revelation is rich in word pictures, or spiritual interpretations. The church is pictured as if it were dwelling in Canaan and re-living the experiences of ancient Israel. Anciently Israel was referred to as "a people near unto Him" (Ps. 148:14), because He reigned in their midst while the gentile world was far removed. This *physical* fact is employed by Paul to *picture* the church as if it were in Palestine and the gentile world "were far off" (Eph. 2:11-22). The Revelator also represents the church as if it were "with Him" "on the mount Sion" (Rev. 14:1). In Rev. 14:20 the destruction of the wicked is symbolized as grapes being trodden in a winepress *"without the city"*—the church is pictured as being safe within the city of Jerusalem. "For *in* mount Zion and *in* Jerusalem shall be deliverance" (Joel 2:32). Satan, seeking to divert the eyes of saints from the assurance contained in the "war" pictures of the final conflict, causes erroneous ideas to be promulgated that these verses have reference to a literal, military conflict in Palestine.

By a spiritual union with Christ believers are *pictured* as being "with Him" (Rev. 17:14) on "mount Sion" (14:1). When the kings of the earth "make *war* with the Lamb" His church is said to be "with Him" (Rev. 17:12-14; 16:14-16; 19:19, 20). Thus the gathering of the nations to "make *war* against the Lamb" and those "with Him" is not a literal gathering of armies, but a portrayal of the final conflict in the form of an imagery, a spiritual application, based upon the conflicts or prophecies of Israel recorded in the Old Testament. The picture of the church dwelling securely within the mighty walls of an impregnable fortress (Prov. 18:10; 2 Sam. 22:3, 51; Isa. 26:1-3, etc.) is the basis of the encouraging imagery of the Apocalypse. The combined forces of the enemy in the last days will not be able to overthrow those who are "more than conquerors through Him that loved us"—this is the spiritual interpretation portrayed in the *symbolic* pictures of the Apocalypse.

The nations who gather to fight against God's people (Zech. 14:12, 13) are *pictured* as being destroyed at Megiddo, where ancient Israel's enemies were *all* destroyed (Judg. 5:19-21; 4:16).

PRINCIPLE NINE:
Observe the Deep, Inner Meaning— Not Alone What Is on the Surface

"**O**ne may read the whole Bible through and yet fail to see its beauty or comprehend its *deep and hidden meaning*" (SC 90). "His words are truth, and they have a *deeper significance* than appears on the surface. All the sayings of Christ have a value beyond their unpretending *appearance*. Minds that are quickened by the Holy Spirit will discern the value of these sayings. They will discern the precious gems of truth, though these may be *buried* treasure" (COL 110). "We do not go *deep enough* in our search for truth. . . . God wants our minds to expand" (TM 119).

"While some portions of the Word are easily understood, the true meaning of other parts is not so readily discerned. There must be patient study and meditation and earnest prayer" (TM 107).

"The truths of the Bible . . . must be searched, *dug out* by painstaking effort" (1SM 20).

"Investigate, compare Scripture with Scripture, sink the shaft of truth down *deep* into the mine of God's Word" (TM 476).

How do we "sink the shaft of truth *deep* into the mine of God's Word" and thus comprehend its "deep and hidden meaning"? The Heavenly injunction for us to "study," "search," "rightly divide," "investigate," "sink," "sink the shaft of truth *deep*" are equated with "compare Scripture with Scripture."

Application:

The spiritual significance of Abraham offering his "*only* son Isaac" on the mountain where, later, Jesus was permitted by His Father to offer Himself as a sacrifice, is obvious. Many times the inner meaning is not so transparently clear. However, the deeper meaning is not to be obtained by some fanciful interpretation. That is not necessary, for somewhere in God's Word will be found the key of explanation. "The entire system of Judaism was a compacted prophecy of the gospel" (DA 211). After His resurrection, Jesus established the faith of His disciples by explaining the "*types* and prophecies of the Old Testament" (DA 796).

When God enjoined the rite of circumcision He inculcated deep spiritual truths (Deut. 10:16, etc.). Paul couples it with conversion and baptism (Col. 2:11-13).

The manna was given to teach "that man doth not live by bread only" (Deut. 8:3), "but by every word that proceedeth out of the mouth of God" (Matt. 4:4). Jesus applied the manna to Himself (John 6), and declared to the Jews that they must *eat* His flesh and *drink* His blood. The Jews "affected to understand His words in the same *literal* sense as did Nicodemus when he asked, 'How can a man be born when he is old?'" (DA 389). Jesus meant that they must receive Him as a personal Saviour and *eat His words*, and thus find eternal life—which is the spiritual meaning explained by Moses (Deut. 8:3). It will be observed that when Satan seeks to hide some deep spiritual truth he causes those deceived to emphasize the literal, thus blinding them to the true significance. It was in this way that Satan led the Jews to reject Christ. The same method of deception may be discerned in the Roman Church. God commanded the Jews to "bind" His words upon their hand, and "as frontlets between thine eyes" (Deut. 6:8). "These words have a *deep meaning*. As the Word of God is meditated upon and practiced, the whole man will be ennobled. In righteous and merciful dealing, the hands will reveal, as a signet, the principles of God's law. . . . But by the Jews of Christ's day all this was undiscerned. The command given to Moses was construed into a direction that the precepts of Scripture should be worn upon the person. They were accordingly written upon strips of parchment, and bound in a conspicuous manner about the head and wrists" (DA 612). The Roman Church continues to employ the literal things of ancient Israel and by doing so, does not understand the spiritual truths, the hidden meaning of the "things" of Israel. Observe the following:

BIBLE PRINCIPLES OF INTERPRETATION

The *Literal* Application by the Roman Catholic Church	The New Testament *Spiritual* Application.
Temple (results in costly churches: "temples of the living God"—they say).	Temple—the Church; believers (1 Cor. 3:16; 2 Cor. 6:16; Eph. 2:21, 22).
Priests.	Priests—on earth, all believers (1 Pet. 2:9).
Incense.	Incense—prayer (Ps. 141:2; Rev. 5:8).
Cross.	Cross—self-denial, daily (Luke 9:23).
Candles.	Light in Temple—Bible (Ps. 119:105; 2 Cor. 4:4).
Bread (Wafer-Mass).	Bread—Word of God (John 6:27, 68).
Water ('Holy water').	Water—Holy Spirit working through Word of God (Titus 3:5; Eph. 5:26).
Fire (Purgatory).	Fire in which dross is burned—(a) Work of the Holy Spirit (Matt. 3:11; Isa. 4:4; 1 Pet. 1:7; 4:12); (b) Obedience to truth purifies (1 Pet. 1:22).
Visible King Visible High Priest } (Pope)	Christ invisible King (1 Tim. 1:17). Christ invisible High Priest (Heb. 8:1; 4:14-16). Holy Spirit is the invisible Head of the Church on earth (John 14:16, 17; 16:7).

The Roman Church by its continuance of the *literal* things of Israel misses the spiritual truths, the hidden meanings, which God intended should be conveyed by their use in the Old Testament.

The New Testament shows the spiritual meaning, and from the many examples given we can readily see that a hidden meaning prevails throughout the Old Testament. John, the writer of the Revelation, was steeped in the use of the deep, inner meaning. When he wrote concerning Judas leaving the upper chamber to betray Jesus: "And it was *night*" (John 13:30), he meant more than that it was night—he referred to the darkness in the soul of Judas (DA 654), for Judas went finally into Satan's kingdom of darkness. When John drew our attention to the number of Christ's miracles—the *first* (John 2:11); then the *second* (John 4:54), he intended us to count how many are recorded in his book—and there is a deep meaning to this. In Rev. 13:18; 17:9-11, John again urges us to use our wisdom in counting. In the gospel of John and in the Revelation a significant use is made of certain numbers.

There is also a deep significance to the catching of the 153 fishes. John says: "After these things Jesus showed Himself *again* to the disciples at the sea of Tiberias" (John 21:1). Here, "by the sea of Galilee," it was that Jesus met with the disciples at the commencement of His ministry and called them "to become fishers of men" (Mark 1:16-18). Before His death Jesus promised to meet them again in *Galilee* (Matt. 26:32; Mark 16:7). Now, after His resurrection, He met with them "*again*" and taught them how to fish—the result being 153 fishes, representing those who will be saved by the gospel net (Matt. 13:47, 48). That morning Jesus served them with their food, as He will do when the gospel net has brought in all the saved (Luke 12:37; Rev. 19:9; EW 19). The word "*Galilee*" signifies a circle, a revolution of a wheel. One circle had been completed, for where He first taught them to be fishers of men He met with them to teach them "*again*" and pointed to the time when the next circle will be completed—when the saved are all gathered to "the marriage supper of the Lamb." The Greek word for *everlasting* is used 17 times in John's gospel, and when numbers one to 17 are counted they make up 153, a symbolic number for all those who will receive *eternal* life. John says that he wrote his gospel "that believing ye might have *life through His* name" (20:31). The gospel of John and the book of Revelation abound with "deep and hidden meanings." "All the sayings of Christ have a value beyond their unpretending appearance. Minds that are quickened by the Holy Spirit will discern the value of these sayings" (COL 110).

PRINCIPLE TEN:
The Design of the Book of Revelation—All the Laws of Interpretation Show That the *Gathering* of the Nations to "Armageddon" Must Commence Before Probation Closes

The Infinite Architect of the Universe is "The Revelator" (Rev. 22:16; GC 342). "This book [Revelation] demands close, prayerful study, lest it be interpreted according to the ideas of men, and false construction be given to the sacred word of the Lord, which in its *symbols* and *figures* means so much to us. . . . In the Revelation the *deep* things of God are portrayed" (*Letter* 16, 1900). "In *figures* and *symbols*, subjects of *vast importance* were presented to John. . . . The *names* of the seven churches are *symbolic*. . . . The *number* seven indicates completeness, and is *symbolic* . . . the *symbols* used" (AA 583-586). "By a variety of *images* the Lord Jesus represented to John" (TM 118). "He [Jesus] sent and *sign*-ified it by His angel unto His servant John" (Rev. 1:1).

"Henry Moore observes 'that there never was a book penned with such artifice as this of the Apocalypse, as if every word were weighed in a balance before it was set down.' . . . Every sentence of it is pregnant with meaning . . . in order to understand its visions, the best method is to examine diligently every word of the Apocalypse"—Bishop Wordsworth.

All the laws of interpretation combine in the Revelation: "In the Revelation all the books of the Bible meet and end" (AA 585). As things mentioned in the early chapters of the Bible are referred to in later books, so, similarly, things mentioned in the early chapters of the Revelation are later referred to in this book. Notice the following examples:

Christ's Second Advent: 1:7; 3:3, 11, 20; 6:14-17; 11:7, 18; 14:14-20; 16:12; 19:11-21.

The wailing and destruction of the wicked: 1:7; 6:14-17; 19:11-21.

The seven stars: 1:16, 20, 13; 2:1.

The first and the last: 1:8, 11, 17; 2:8; 22:13.

A sharp, two-edged sword: 1:14, 15; 2:16; 19:15.

Eyes as a flaming fire: 1:14; 2:18; 19:12.

The seven Spirits: 1:4; 3:1; 4:5; 5:6.

The faithful Witness: 1:5; 3:14; 19:11.

The true Witness: 1:5; 3:14; 19:11; 22:6.

Jews: 2:9; 7:1-8; 14:1; 21:12.

Saints have power over the nations: 2:26, 27; 17:14; 20: 4.

White raiment: 3:5, 18; 6:11; 7:14; 16:15; 19:8.

Door of sanctuary shut: 3:7, 8; 11:19; 15:5-8; 16.

The synagogue of Satan: 2:9; 13:6, 8, 14-18, etc.

Where Satan's seat is: 2:13; 13:3; 18:2.

The holy city: 3:12; 11:1; 14:20; 21:22.

Kings and priests: 1:6; 5:10; 20:4.

The kings of the earth: 1:5, 6; 6:15; 16:14; 17:12-14; 19:19.

Thus we see illustrated in the Revelation the principle of employing again that which has been mentioned previously. By repetitions of the seed thought presented in Rev. 1:7, the Revelator works towards the great climax in the struggle between the forces of God and of Satan—the slaughter of the enemies of spiritual Israel in the antitypical Megiddo conflict.

All the prophetic places, proper names, and designations of the Revelation are employed *symbolically*: the 7 cities "in Asia" (Rev. 1:11), Jews, Israel, Antipas, Balaam, Jezebel, the names of the 12 tribes of Israel, Egypt, Sodom, the Holy City (Rev. 11:1), the Temple (Rev. 11:1), Sion, Euphrates, Hebrew, Armageddon, Babylon, Gog and Magog. Thus we see that the general design of the Revelation is to use places and proper names in a *symbolic* sense. The first time *"place"* is used (Rev. 2:5) it refers to Ephesus, a city "in Asia"—not so very far removed from Megiddo—consequently the same word in Rev. 16:16 also refers to a *symbolic* "place." In *Our Firm Foundation*, Vol. 2, pp. 291, 292, it is stated: "The *Ar* at the beginning of the word translated `Armageddon' in the Authorized Version should be *Har*, and is so found in a number of English versions. . . . *Har* is the Hebrew word for 'Mountain,' and it is so rendered nearly 500 times in the Old Testament. If we consider *Har* as `mountain' and the remainder of the word, *mageddon*, the same as the 'Megiddo' of the Old Testament, we have the meaning—`mountain of Megiddo.' But was there such a mountain? We do find in the Old Testament written references to: The city of Megiddo (1 Kings 9:15); the plain of Megiddo (Zech. 12:11, LXX); the waters of Megiddo (Judg. 5:19); the king of Megiddo (Josh. 17:11); the valley of Megiddo (2 Chron. 35:22). . . . But there was no hill or mountain bearing that name. This is recognized by many students of prophecy, as the previous excerpts show. This being the case, we are forced to think of this word in a symbolic sense."

As "Armageddon" is employed symbolically in a world-wide sense, the Euphrates, which is mentioned in the same description, must also have a worldwide symbolic sense.

The Revelation is based upon the principle that the world-wide is symbolized by the local. In the commencement of this book we read that Jesus "hath made us *kings and priests*" (l:6). Thus the designation of the king-priest of Salem (Melchisedec), the type of Christ, is applied to believers (who share the privilege of ministry and service with their Lord). The quotation in Rev. 1:7: "All kindreds of the earth shall wail because of Him" takes us back to Zech. 12:11-14 where this *mourning* of the "*families*" (tribes) was said to occur "*in Jerusalem*, as the mourning of Hadadrimmon *in the valley of Megiddon*." When quoting this passage of Zechariah in predicting the worldwide scenes associated with His Second Advent, Jesus said: "Then shall all the *tribes* of the earth *mourn*" (Matt. 24:30). John's application of the same verses in Zechariah is, "All kindreds [or 'tribes'] *of the earth* shall wail because of Him." It is to these same worldwide "tribes"—"every kindred"—that the message of Rev. 14:6 is being heralded. Thus the Revelation employs the principle that the worldwide is symbolized in the local—and that is how he brings into his pictures of the worldwide Armageddon the Old Testament events and places, including Megiddo.

The Revelator Employs the Principle that Old Testament Local Types have a Worldwide Application.

No one can understand God's last-day Message without first studying carefully into the typical services of the day of atonement—no one can understand the Revelator's reference to the Judgment-hour Message (Rev. 14:6, 7) unless he first studies Israel's national economy regarding the closing work of the High Priest in the typical services. No one can understand the Revelator's statement concerning the second angel's message: "Babylon is fallen, is fallen, that great city" (Rev. 14:8) if he has not first studied the Old Testament record concerning the fall of Babylon by Cyrus, who dried up the waters of the Euphrates to obtain an entrance into Babylon, which led to its overthrow. Rev. 14:8 is the first time the Revelator mentioned anything about Babylon. The Revelation is the most scientifically written Book in all the world. It was written by the infinite Law-Giver, the Omniscient Creator, the Almighty Redeemer—and He wrote it *for His church* (Rev. 22:16). Bishop Wordsworth says: "Henry Moore observes 'that there never was a book penned with such artifice as this of the Apocalypse, as if every word were weighed in a balance before it was set down.' These remarkable specimens of careful composition in its earlier chapters may have been designed to remind the reader, that every sentence of it is pregnant with meaning, and that in order to understand its Visions, the best method is to examine diligently every word of the Apocalypse." The servant of the Lord has cautioned us with regard to the study of the Revelation: "This book demands *close*, prayerful study, *lest it be interpreted according to the ideas of men, and false construction* be given to the sacred word of the Lord, which in its *symbols* and *figures* means so much to *us*. . . . In the Revelation the *deep* things of God are portrayed" (Letter 16, 1900).

In the Apocalypse, "the wonderful Numberer" (Dan. 8:13, margin) mentions the word "Babylon" 6 times. The image set up by the king of ancient Babylon was 60 cubits high, and 6 cubits in breadth (Dan. 3:1). At the dedication of this image 6 kinds of music were used (Dan. 3:5, 10, 15). Belshazzar praised 6 gods (Dan. 5:4). Other verses in Daniel designedly emphasize the number 6. In the

Revelation, "Babylon" is mentioned 6 times (14:8; 16:19; 17:5; 18:2, 10, 21). The woman representing the church of Babylon, is mentioned 6 times (17:3, 4, 6, 7, 9, 18). Six things are associated with her dress (Rev. 17:4). The same number is made up in Rev. 18:16. Six times Babylon's "fornication" is referred to (2:21; 14:8; 17:2, 4; 18:3; 19:2). The voices of 6 persons will not be heard in her again (18:22, 23). Six times it is said of the things of Babylon, that they shall be "no more at all" (18:14, 21-23). The 1,000 years of desolation are mentioned 6 times (Rev. 20:2-7), which shows that the destruction is Babylon's. Other numbers relating to Babylon, such as the 666 of Rev. 13:18, will readily come to mind. Thus there is evidence of *design* in the way the things of Babylon are brought to view in the Revelation.

The intricate pattern woven with words which follow the first mention of Babylon (14:8), depends upon the key provided in that first mention. How does the All-wise Revelator explain the principle to be employed when seeking to interpret His references to Babylon? He introduces the theme of Babylon by the words: "Babylon is fallen, is fallen, that great city, because she made all nations drink of the wine of the wrath of her fornication." He does not say: "This refers to *spiritual* Babylon," because the principle has already been given throughout the New Testament following the rejection of the Jewish nation— that all the things pertaining to Israel and her enemies now belong to the church and her enemies. And our Lord, in referring to the fall of Babylon, intended His remnant people to go back to the Old Testament passages which He quotes—see Isa. 21:9; Jer. 51:8; Dan. 4:30; etc. Thus our infinite Lord has given the key to the understanding of the Revelation—go back to the Old Testament for the local setting and then apply that in a *worldwide application in connection with His church* in the last days. To interpret the drying up of the Euphrates and the coming of the kings of the east to refer to modern *local* nations like Turkey and nations to the east of Palestine, means to ignore the Revelator's *designed* interpretation concerning the worldwide application and also the more important principle that these things must be understood *in relation to His church*—"to *us*," as the Lord's servant has stated it in the quotation given above. See also the following statement: "*When* we as a people understand what this book means to *us*, there will be seen among *us* a great revival" (TM 113). "*When*" this principle of interpretation is appreciated, it will cause God's people to obtain such spiritual food from the study of "the books of Daniel and Revelation" that this will bring about *"a great revival"*—"believers will have an *entirely different religious experience*" (TM 114).

The Revelator wrote to those who know the Old Testament where the taking of Babylon by Cyrus (and other "kings" "from the east") is fully described. No one can fully understand the Revelation without first becoming acquainted with the prophecies and the historical events to which He so frequently refers. As the Revelator has already made reference in Rev. 14:8 to the overthrow of Babylon, His reference in Rev. 16:12 to the coming of "the kings from the east" and the drying up of the Euphrates must be understood in the light of His previous reference to the fall of Babylon. Only those who have gone back to the Old Testament to study the fall of Babylon will understand His reference in Rev. 16:12. Rev. 16:12-16 should be interpreted in the light of the Old Testament type and the worldwide antitype for that is the principle upon which the three-fold Message of Rev. 14:6-12 is established.

No one can see the significance of God's warning against worshipping the beast and his image, without seeing the Revelator's antitypical application of the three faithful Hebrews who refused to bow to the image set up by the king of Babylon (compare Dan. 3:5, 7, 10, 12, 14, 18 with Rev. 13:15; 14:9, 11; 16:2; 19:20; 20:4). What was literal and local then is worldwide and spiritual in the last days. In the typical experience the King of Babylon commanded all to obey or be killed. In the antitypical decree of the king of spiritual Babylon all will be commanded to obey the decree of the State to worship the spiritual image in spiritual Babylon or be killed—this is the application made by the Spirit of Prophecy of this Old Testament experience (PK 512, 513).

All the Laws of Interpretation show that the *Gathering of the Nations to Armageddon* must commence before probation closes.

It has been shown that the drying of waters of the Euphrates refers back to the overthrow of ancient Babylon by Cyrus. It has also been shown that the places mentioned in the prophecies of the Revelation are employed symbolically in a worldwide sense in connection with Christ's kingdom or the kingdom of

Satan—hence Armageddon has a worldwide significance. It has been shown that the first battle fought at Megiddo as recorded in the Old Testament, is where ancient Israel triumphed over their oppressors, so the Revelator's antitypical reference could refer only to the final conflict where Israel's enemies, seeking to destroy them, are themselves destroyed. The reference to "the *Hebrew*" shows the conflict concerns *Hebrews* who have come out of Babylon. It has also been shown that names are employed significantly in the prophecies of the Revelation because of their meaning. It is because "Armageddon" means "the mountain of slaughter," or destruction, that it is employed as a symbolic word to describe the destruction of those who have joined with Satan in his rebellion against the Government of God. Thus Rev. 16:12-16 can be understood only in a worldwide sense in connection with the church and her enemies.

There are other laws of interpretation which lead us to the same conclusion, and it is a corollary drawn from this fact that emphasizes the solemn truth that *The Gathering to Armageddon Precedes the 6th Plague*.

The *gathering* to Armageddon is the key to the understanding of the prophecies depicting the final conflict. The *gathering* undoubtedly commences *before probation closes* and reaches its culmination before the 6th plague. By principles of interpretation we may be positively certain that the gathering envisaged in Rev. 16:13-15 does *not* occur *after* the drying up of the Euphrates (Rev. 16:12)—it simply *could not possibly occur after that mighty event*. These verses teach that the gathering must commence before probation closes. It cannot be too strongly stated that the gathering of "the kings of the earth and of the whole world" could *not* possibly occur after the drying up of the Euphrates and MUST commence before probation closes. The day is not far distant when this mighty truth will be proclaimed by the (SDA) Church—both the Bible and the Spirit of Prophecy make this very clear. This is the prophetic proclamation of the Loud Cry. The people of the whole world will be informed that they must choose to take their stand either on God's side or on Satan's before probation closes and the plagues fall.

When the *gathering* to Armageddon is understood, everything else just falls into its proper place. The Spirit of Prophecy teaches that the gathering commences before probation closes, yes, and has already commenced: "*Already* the inhabitants of the earth are marshalling under the leading of the prince of darkness, and this is but the beginning of the end" (8T 49; see also p. 307). "The *present* is a solemn, fearful time for the church. The angels are already girded, awaiting the mandate of God to pour their vials of wrath upon the world. . . . Satan is also mustering his forces of evil, *going forth* 'unto the kings of the earth and of the whole world,' to gather them under his banner, to be *trained* for 'the battle of that great day of God Almighty.' Satan is to make most powerful efforts for the mastery in the last great conflict. . . . The faith of individual members of the church will be tested as though there were not another person in the world" (Ms 1a, 1890; 7BC 983). "There are only *two parties in our world*, those who are loyal to God, and those who stand under the banner of the prince of darkness. . . . The battle of Armageddon is soon to be fought. He on whose vesture is written the name, King of kings and Lord of lords, leads forth the armies of heaven on white horses, clothed in fine linen, clean and white" (Ms 172, 1899; 7BC 982). "Evil angels . . . will not yield the last great final contest without a desperate struggle. *All the world* will be on one side or the other of the question. The battle of Armageddon will be fought. And that day must find none of us sleeping. Wide awake *we* must be, as wise virgins having oil in our vessels with our lamps. The power of the Holy Ghost must be upon us and the Captain of the Lord's hosts will stand at the head of the angels of heaven to direct the battle" (Letter 109, 1890; 7BC 982). "*We* need to study the pouring out of the seventh vial. The powers of evil will not yield up the conflict without a struggle. But Providence has a part to act in the battle of Armageddon. When the earth is lighted with the glory of the angel of Revelation eighteen, the religious elements, good and evil, will awake from slumber, and the armies of the living God will take the field" (Ms 175, 1899; 7BC 983).

These extracts definitely teach that the *gathering* to the battle of that great day of God Almighty has already occurred and that that gathering will gather momentum when the Loud Cry is given. In GC 561, 562, the Lord's servant quotes Rev. 16:13, 14 and applies these verses to events happening before probation closes. After quoting Rev. 16:13, 14 concerning the gathering of the kings of the earth and the whole world, she says: "Except those who are kept by the power of God, through faith in His word, the whole world will be swept into the ranks of this delusion. The people are fast being lulled to a fatal security, to be awakened only by *the outpouring of the wrath of God*"—thus the *gathering* mentioned in Rev. 16:13-14 is applied to events occurring before probation closes. Through spiritualism Satan gathers the world under his banner—the only ones who will not be gathered into his forces are "those who are kept by the power of God, through faith in His word." The same truth is stated in TM 465: "The enmity of Satan against good will be manifested more and more as he brings his forces into activity in his last work of rebellion; and *every soul* that is not *fully surrendered* to God, and *kept* by divine power, will form an alliance with Satan against Heaven, and join in battle against the Ruler of the universe."

Thus there can be no mistaking the fact that the Spirit of Prophecy definitely teaches that the gathering to the battle of that great day of God Almighty, which culminates in Armageddon, *has already commenced*—never once does the Lord's servant apply the gathering to any event supposed to occur after the drying up of the Euphrates: such a teaching is without support from either the Bible or the Spirit of Prophecy. The Lord's servant states emphatically that "The written testimonies are not to give new light, but to impress vividly upon the heart the truths of inspiration *already revealed*. . . . Additional truth is not brought out; but God has through the Testimonies simplified the great truths *already given*" (5T 665). Therefore the gathering of Rev. 16:13, 14 as explained by her, must be the actual teaching of the Scriptures.

When the Lord's servant describes events particularly during the Loud Cry, she employs such words as, *"war," "conflict," "struggle," "controversy," "battle,"* and pictures God's people as *"soldiers"* with *"armor."* "In vision I saw two *armies* in terrible *conflict* . . . a mighty *General* cried out with a loud voice: 'Come into line. Let those who are loyal . . . now take their position. Come out from among them. . . . the *battle* raged. . . . Christ's *soldiers* . . . the *army* following the banner with the inscription,

'The Commandments of God, and the faith of Jesus,' was gloriously triumphant. . . . Men have confederated to *oppose* the Lord of hosts" (8T 41, 42; GC 592; EW 271; PK 725, etc.). "The Sabbath question is to be *the* issue in the great final conflict in which all the world will act a part" (6T 352).

As Moses declared to the Egyptians that their stand against God and His people would bring upon them the plagues (Ex. 4:23; 7:4, 5; 8:2, 21; 9:2, 3, 13-16; 10:4, 20, 21; 11:1), so the world will be warned that by taking their stand against God's Government the plagues (Rev. 16) will fall upon them. They will be urged to take their stand with Christ's army— or receive God's judgments. "It is not until the issue is thus *plainly set before the people.* . . . Men are not to be left in darkness concerning this *important* matter; the warning against this sin is *to be given to the world before the visitation of God's judgments, that all may know why* they are *to be* inflicted, and have opportunity to escape them" (GC 449, 450; 9T 20; DA 634). In the Loud Cry the "Armageddon" message, far from being estimated as a relatively minor subject, will be borne as *the* important message for the hour and proclaimed with mighty power: stand with the Lord's loyal army—or be destroyed in "Armageddon."

Why does the Lord's servant say that "*we need* to study the pouring out of the seventh vial" and connect up that study with the Loud Cry? Because it is under the Loud Cry that the people of the world either gather for or against Christ in the great controversy. After quoting Rev. 18:2, 4, the Lord's servant says: "Soon the last test is to come to all the inhabitants of the earth. At that time *prompt decisions will be made*" (9T 149). "In the issue of the conflict all Christendom will be divided into two great classes" (9T 16; see also GC 605; COL 283). "They [God's people under the Loud Cry] were clothed with an *armor* from their head to their feet. They moved in exact order, *like a company of soldiers.* . . . I heard those clothed with the *armor* speak forth the truth with great power" (EW 271). "Clad in the *armor* of Christ's righteousness, the church is to enter upon her final conflict. 'Fair as the moon, clear as the sun, and *terrible as an army* with banners' (Song of Sol. 6:10), she is to go forth into all the world, conquering and to conquer. The darkest hour of the church's struggle with the powers of evil is that which immediately *precedes the day of her final deliverance*" (PK 725). Here, again, the Lord's servant links the proclamation of the Loud Cry with the *deliverance* which comes to God's people under the 6th and 7th plagues. The 7th plague commences with the voice of God saying *"It is done"* (Rev. 16:17), and those words mean that God's people are *delivered from persecution*; the power of Satan's armies "to annoy them is gone forever" (1T 354, 184; GC 640; EW 15, 285). Those who made "war with the Lamb" *"in the person of His witnesses"* (7T 182)—"The final struggle *against Christ and His followers*" (GC 593)—will be destroyed in "Armageddon," "the mount of slaughter."

Writing of the *"Deliverance* of the Saints," the Lord's servant says that after they are delivered by God's voice "There was a mighty shout of victory *over the beast and over his image*" (EW 285, 286), which further shows that the mighty conflict with the beast, his image, and his mark, which commences in earnest with the Loud Cry, ends with the deliverance of modern Israel by God's voice at the opening of the 7th plague—hence the reason for the inspired counsel for us to connect up the Loud Cry with the intervention of God Almighty in the battle of Armageddon, *the slaughter of the enemies of God's people.*

Describing the time "when the voice of God turns the captivity of His people," the Lord's servant says that the people turn upon their "spiritual guardians": "The swords which were to slay God's people are now employed to destroy *their enemies.* Everywhere there is strife and bloodshed. . . . In the mad strife of their own fierce passions, and by the awful outpouring of God's unmingled wrath, fall the wicked inhabitants of the earth—priests, rulers, and people, rich and poor, high and low. 'And the *slain of the Lord* shall be at that day from one end of the earth even unto the other end of the earth' (Jer. 25:33)" (GC 654-657).

God's servant says: "We are told of *a greater battle* to take place in the closing scenes of earth's history. . . . The Revelator describes *the destruction that is to take place when the `great* voice *out of the temple of heaven' announces, `It is done'*" (PP 509). Under the 7th plague "great Babylon" comes "in remembrance before God, to give unto her the cup of the wine of the fierceness of His wrath."

Revelation 17 was written to explain how "Babylon the Great" would be destroyed: "And there came one of the seven angels which had the seven vials, and talked with me, saying unto me, Come hither; I will show unto thee the judgment of the great whore *that sitteth upon many waters*" (v. 1), which is a quotation from Jer. 51:13—see the marginal reference. Turning to Jer. 51:13 we read: "O thou [Babylon, see v. 12] that *dwellest upon many waters*, abundant in treasures, *thine end is come*." Jer. 50:38 is the verse referred to in Rev. 16:12 (see margins in both), and it reads: "A drought is upon her [*Babylon's waters*]; and *they shall be dried up* . . . and it shall be no more inhabited." Thus the drying up of the waters of the Euphrates mentioned in Rev. 16:12, points to *the ending of the power of Babylon*. It was prophesied of ancient Babylon: "Desolation shall come upon thee *suddenly*" (Isa. 47:11); "Babylon is *suddenly* fallen and destroyed" (Jer. 51:8). In the darkness of the night Cyrus deflected the waters of the Euphrates, entered Babylon, and overthrew its government (Isa. 44:27, 28; 45:1; see PK 531, 549). "In *that night* was Belshazzar the king of the Chaldeans slain." Similarly, modern Babylon, the persecutors of God's people will be suddenly overthrown. The Lord's servant links together the plague of *darkness* (5th plague)—see GC 635, 636—with the voice of God that delivers His people at the opening of the 7th plague. That is, the darkness falls, the rainbow—the sign of the covenant, which is connected in Scripture with the 6th plague—and the *commencement* of the 7th plague occur together the same night as one picture of the deliverance of God's people. As in PK 531, 549 the deliverance of ancient Israel was brought about by the drying up of the waters of the Euphrates, so spiritual Israel will be delivered by the drying up of the waters of the Euphrates. Writing of events to occur after the fourth plague, the Lord's servant says: "The end will come more quickly than men expect" (GC 631). It would be beyond the scope of this outline to go deeply into the matter, but there will not be sufficient time *after* the drying up of the Euphrates for the *gathering* of the nations. When Babylonian leaders are revealed as false shepherds there will be "strife and bloodshed" everywhere (GC 642, 656). Then all the weapons of warfare will be employed. The dreadful slaughter of "Armageddon" comes after the drying up of the waters of the Euphrates (study Rev. 17:15-17), but the *gathering* commences before probation closes and reaches its culmination before the 6th plague—this is the teaching of Rev. 16:12-21, and of the Spirit of Prophecy.

Question:

Who leads or gathers the nations to the slaughter of Armageddon?

Answer:

Rev. 16:13, 14: Evil spirits working through the Dragon, the Beast, and the False Prophet.

Question:

Against whom do the Beast, the False Prophet, and Kings gather?

Answer:

"I saw the beast, and the kings of the earth, and their armies, gathered together to make war *against Him that sat on the horse, and against His army*" (Rev. 19:19, 20). The beast and the false prophet are brought into the apocalyptic visions because they enforce "the mark of the beast" (v. 20), which is an institution of the apostate *church*. They are religious powers leading out in a religious war working through the States. "Under one head—the papal power—the people will unite to oppose God in the person of His witnesses" (7T 182). "The final struggle *against Christ and His followers*" (GC 593). "These shall make *war with the Lamb*, and the Lamb shall overcome them" (Rev. 17:14). It is evident from the fact that the beast and the false prophet lead out in this "war"—a Papal-Protestant union—against *"Christ and His followers,"* that the Revelator does not depict a military war.

Our *Bible Commentary*, vol. 4, 295, says: "In the last days also there will be, on the part of all the hosts of evil, a united, but unsuccessful, effort for the destruction of the saints (see Rev. 16:14-16; 19:11-21)."

Question:

What is represented by the *Dragon*?

Answer:

The States—(see TM 39) *"Kings, rulers, and governors . . . are represented* as the dragon who goes to make war with the saints."

Louis F. Were

Question:

When and How do they "make war with the saints?"

Answer:

"In the soon-coming conflict [over the enforcement of Sunday laws] we shall see exemplified the prophet's words: 'The *dragon* was wroth with the woman, and went to make *war* with the remnant of her seed, which keep the commandments of God. . . .' (Rev. 12:17)" (GC 592).

This "war" commences before probation closes. The Loud Cry is God's message against this action by "the powers of earth, *uniting* [*gathering*] to war against the commandments of God" (GC 604, etc.), giving solemn warning of the fearful consequences that will eventuate as the outcome (Rev. 18:1-8).

That the dragon refers to the earthly governments, the kings, may be discerned by comparing Rev. 16:13, 14 with Rev. 19:19, 20. In these verses there are three powers that gather the world to war upon the Government of Heaven, and Rev. 19:19, 20 is explicit in declaring that the "*miracles*" or "*signs*" mentioned in Rev. 16:14; 13:13, 14, are those employed to deceive people concerning "the mark of the beast." Rev. 16:13 mentions *the dragon*, beast, and false prophet: Rev. 19:19, 20 mentions the *kings* of the earth, the beast and the false prophet. In Rev. 16:13, 14 the dragon is mentioned first because the religious powers can make war on God's people only when the State passes laws inimical to them. Thus the State becomes the spearhead of the attack. Revelation 17 was written to explain that the Babylonian whore rides the States to do her bidding. In this prophecy it is the "*kings*" who "make war with the Lamb, and the Lamb shall overcome them" (v. 12-14). "Fearful is the issue to which the world is to be brought. *The powers of earth*, uniting to war against the commandments of God, will decree . . ." (GC 604).

The "*miracles*" that "*gather*" "the kings of the earth and of the whole world" are performed to prove (?) that Sunday should be observed, see GC 590, 591, 612, etc. This is done before probation closes: "Fearful sights of a supernatural character will soon be revealed in the heavens, in token of the power of miracle-working demons. The spirits of devils will go forth to the kings of the earth and to the whole world, to fasten them in deception, and urge them on to unite with Satan in his last struggle against the government of heaven. By these agencies, *rulers* and *subjects* will be alike deceived. . . . As the crowning act in the great drama of deception, Satan himself will personate Christ. . . . Now the great deceiver will make it appear that Christ has come . . . he claims to have changed the Sabbath to Sunday. . . . He declares that those who persist in keeping holy the seventh day are blaspheming his name by refusing to listen to his angels sent to them with light and truth" (GC 624). The personal appearance of Satan occurs *before probation closes*—see GC 593; TM 62, etc. Thus we see that the Lord's servant applies the gathering of the kings of the earth and of the whole world through the miracles performed by evil spirits as not only being commenced before probation closes, but also that this gathering is interpreted to mean the passing of State laws making it unlawful to obey God's law, thus causing war against God's Government, which leads to the destruction of His opponents.

The resurgent Papacy inviting Christendom to unite, and many so-called Protestants seeking unity with the Papacy, will bring the world into that place where it will make war "against Christ and his followers." "The final movements will be rapid ones."

Why *Literal* Water in the 2nd and 3rd plagues (Rev. 16:3, 4) and yet *Symbolic* Water in v. 12?

This is a challenging problem for which those who apply Rev. 16:12-16 in a literal-Megiddo-or-Palestinian sense have no answer. The waters of the Euphrates are interpreted *symbolically* whether applied to Turkey or to the people of Babylon. The application to Turkey is guesswork. There can be no doubt that the waters of the Euphrates symbolize "peoples, and multitudes, and nations, and tongues" who do the bidding of Babylon in persecuting God's people, for this is exactly how the angel explained it—see Rev. 17:1, 15.

To understand this problem—concerning *literal* water in Rev. 16:3, 4, and yet *symbolic* water in v. 12—we must study the design employed in the Revelation. The Revelator, in His other uses of the number seven, divides 7 into 4 and 3. This is clearly seen in the "7 seals" (Rev. 6) and in the "7 trumpets" (Rev. 8; 9; 11:15). *Four* of the *seals* feature horses—the four horses of the

Apocalypse —then 3 *seals* with other features describing events leading to the Second Advent. The four *trumpets* are distinguished from the 3 "*woe* trumpets" which bring us down to the Second Advent. In the messages to the "7 churches" the same division of 4 and 3 is revealed. In Rev. 2:7, 11, 17 each of the 3 promises is *preceded* by, "He that hath an ear let him hear what the Spirit saith unto the churches." But in Rev. 2:29; 3:6, 13, 22 each of the 4 promises is *followed* by that same phrase: "He that hath an ear, let him hear what the Spirit saith unto the churches." Thus there is an obvious system employed in the series of sevens that lead to the coming of Christ—the number 7 is divided into 4 and 3. In the study of the "7 churches" the last 4 emphasize the approach of the Second Advent: Hold fast till I come (2:25); I will come as a thief (3:3); I come quickly (3:11); I stand at the door (3:20).

Now we are better able to understand why the Spirit of Prophecy, after very briefly (on *only one* page) dealing with the first 4 plagues, says: "*These* plagues are not universal" (GC 628) thus distinguishing them from the 3 later plagues that will be universal. Before dealing with the last 3 plagues she says: "The end will come more quickly than men expect" (p. 631). The last 3 plagues burst upon the world in one night, with the destruction of the Babylonian kingdom continuing on for the few days that remain until the coming of Christ. As in the divisions of the previous sevens—7 churches, 7 seals, 7 trumpets—into 4 and 3 with the last division emphasizing the hastening to the Second Advent, so the last 3 plagues announce that the end has come. There is a distinct division between the first 4 plagues and the last 3. The first 4 deal with the judgments that fall upon the nations for forbidding the keeping of the true Sabbath, and for their treatment of God's people; the last 3 deal specifically with the destruction of Babylon. That is, the religious elements will control the nations until just a few days before the Second Advent—Babylon sits upon the waters of the Euphrates (peoples, multitudes, nations, tongues) until the 6th plague, at which time those that supported her persecutions suddenly turn upon her when God intervenes to deliver His people (Rev. 17:13-18). As Cyrus in the darkness dried up the waters of the Euphrates, so the darkness of the 5th plague falls, and the multitudes turn against their religious leaders—the waters no longer serve Babylon, but become an avenue for her destruction. The first 4 plagues will be similar to the plagues that fell upon *Egypt* (GC 627). *Egypt*, in the Bible, is a *symbol of State* or national power—*not* a symbol of church power: "No *monarch* ever ventured upon more open and highhanded rebellion against the *authority* of Heaven than did the *king* of Egypt . . . and the *nation* represented by Egypt would give voice to a similar denial of the claims of the living God and would manifest a like spirit of unbelief and defiance" (GC 269).

Christ commences His reign as "*King* of kings" before He leaves the most holy place. At the close of His priestly ministry He receives His kingdom, and then begins to reign as "*King* of kings" (EW 280, 281; GC 428) before the plagues are poured out.

"At that time shall Michael *stand up* [having completed His priestly work, He then commences to exercise His authority as King to defend His people and to deal with His enemies] . . . and there shall be a time of trouble, such as never was since there was a *nation*" (Dan. 12:1; Ps. 2:1-9; Rev. 11:15-18). "Jesus is about to leave the mercy seat of the heavenly sanctuary to put on garments of vengeance and pour out His wrath in judgments upon those who have not responded to the light God has given them. . . . The Infinite One still keeps an account with all *nations*. . . . The *nations* of this age. . . . The Lord comes forth as an avenger" (5T 207-210). "When the *rulers* of the land will rank themselves on the side of the man of sin—it is then the measure of guilt is full. The *national* apostasy is the signal for *national* ruin" (2SM 373; 5T 451). "The law of God will . . . be made void in our land; and *national* apostasy will be followed by *national* ruin" (RH, Dec. 18, 1888). "Then there will be a law against the Sabbath of God's creation, and then it is that God 'will do a strange work in the earth'" (RH, Mar. 9, 1886). "When this substitution [Sunday in place of the Sabbath "by merely human *authority*"] becomes universal, God will reveal Himself. He will arise in His *majesty* to shake terribly the earth" (7T 141).

The Spirit of Prophecy differentiates between the plagues resembling Egypt, which occur before the deliverance of God's people (GC 627, 628), and those which fall in connection with their deliverance. In Chapter 40: *"God's People Delivered"* is mentioned the darkness (5th plague) that *"falls upon the earth"* that commences that deliverance. On the same page (636) reference is made to the commencement of the 7th plague—the midnight hour when "God manifests His power for the deliverance of His people." Thus the Spirit of Prophecy places a division between the first 4 plagues already dealt with on page 628, and the last 3 plagues which are later mentioned in the chapter *"God's People Delivered."* The first 4 plagues are said to resemble those that fell upon Egypt (p. 628), and it is these that are said to fall *before the deliverance of God's people* (p. 627, 628). The Lord's servant deals with the first 4 plagues which fall upon the governments for their part in persecuting the people of God and in defying His authority as Lawgiver; then she applies the last 3 plagues in connection with the overthrow of dominating religious leaders and the destruction of Babylon. *Egypt represents kingly* power as distinguished from the Babylonian or religious power. God punishes the States by the first 4 plagues for passing laws forbidding the keeping of the Sabbath. Babylon dominates the nations until the time has come for the unmasking of the mystery of iniquity in connection with the drying up of the Euphrates. Then the people who support her will destroy their religious leaders (Rev. 17:15-17; Jer. 25:34-38). Of the first 4 plagues we read: *"These* plagues are not universal, or the inhabitants of the earth would be wholly cut off" (GC 628). But that cannot be said of the last 3 plagues, for they will be sent to wholly cut off all the inhabitants of the earth.

Because the Euphrates is Babylon's river and *Babylon is symbolic*, the waters of the Euphrates *must also be symbolic*—the context demands this. However, as the first 4 plagues are not said specifically to be poured out upon Babylon as such but upon Egypt-like *nations and governments*, the context does not require that the waters of the 2nd and 3rd plagues be symbolically understood.

THE REVELATOR'S DESIGN IN USING "I SAW" IN REV. 16:13

There is a principle operating throughout the Apocalypse to guide the reader when to make a break in the continuity of the events described. Obviously, verses 13-15 of Rev. 16 do not follow in chronological sequence after v. 12 and by the words *"And I saw,"* the Revelator deliberately designed that this fact should be noted. The prophecy of Rev. 16:13-15 refers to events commencing *before* probation closes—the two classes of mankind preparing to receive the seal of God or the mark of the beast. The Spirit of Prophecy plainly employs Rev. 16:15 in connection with *character preparation* for the close of probation—see COL 319; DA 636; Rev. 16:13-15 proclaims the Lord's earnest warning for His people to get ready for the close of probation. Our *SDA Bible Commentary*, vol. 7, p. 766 says that when the Revelator uses the words *"I saw,"* He does so "to introduce *new scenes or important new symbols."* Thus our Lord in Rev. 16:13 stresses the importance of this prophecy and deliberately draws attention to the fact that there is a break in the continuity of the events described, that verses 13-15 actually *precede* the drying up of the Euphrates (v. 12). The *gathering* to Armageddon (vs. 13-15) commences before probation closes. The decisions made before probation closes will determine whether or not we shall be destroyed in Armageddon, and this is the significance of breaking the continuity or sequence of events in vs. 13-15.

PRINCIPLE ELEVEN:
New Testament Principles Determine the Interpretation of the Latter Portion of Daniel 11

S ome have concluded that as the first part of Daniel 11 deals with literal or national, military wars around Jerusalem, so the ending of the prophecy must likewise refer to military wars near or around Jerusalem. However, this line of reasoning is contrary to the Scriptures. All SDA expositors agree that the Papacy is brought into the prophecy from verse 31 and onwards. The persecutions of God's people in Europe, the wearing out of the saints during the 1260 years of Papal supremacy (Dan. 7:25), are brought to view in Dan. 11:33-35. In Dan. 8:9 Rome (in its twofold character: Pagan and Papal) is said to come from the West. When Paul quotes from Dan. 11:36 (see marginal references) and applies this prophecy to "that man of sin, the son of perdition" (2 Thess. 2:3), he says that this power "as God sitteth in the temple of God, showing himself that he is God." Jerusalem was the only place where God commanded that His temple be built (Deut. 12:5, 11, 14, 18, 21, 26; 1 Chron. 21:18, 28; 22:1, 2; 2 Chron. 3:1). This Western power, this European "king," which persecuted God's people *in Europe*, Paul declared was to sit *"in the temple of God,"* and the only place where the *literal* temple could be built was in Jerusalem. Obviously, then, according to New Testament principles, Daniel's prophecy concerning the king of the north and the temple in Jerusalem, is not to be understood in a literal-Jerusalem setting. By the term *"the temple of God"* the inspired Paul referred to the Christian church, see 1 Cor. 3:16; 2 Cor. 6:16; Eph. 2:22; etc. The Lord Jesus, in Rev. 11:1, 2, employs the term "temple" and "the holy city" to refer to His church.

The book of Daniel was explicitly written for God's people living in "the time of the end" (Dan. 12:4, 9), especially since

1844, when added light came in regard to the antitypical application of the things of Israel. The transition from the literal geographical setting to the "church" application, which operates in Daniel's last vision—an explanation of his previous ones— also occurs in his other prophecies. His prophecy of chapter Two commenced in literal Babylon and passes to spiritual Babylon centered in Europe. Concerning the prophecy of "the feet of the image in which iron was mixed with miry clay," the Lord's servant says: "But statesmen will uphold the spurious Sabbath. . . . The mingling of churchcraft and statecraft is represented by the iron and the clay. This union is weakening all the power of the churches. This investing the church with the power of the state will bring evil results. Men . . . have invested their strength in politics, and have united with the Papacy . . ." (4BC 1168, 1169). Daniel's subsequent prophecies are enlargements of this prophecy concerning the image, with particular emphasis upon the Roman power in its two-fold aspects, especially with reference to Papal Rome. The same transition that occurs in Dan. 2 may be observed in the following prophecies of Daniel. Our Lord Jesus applied this same principle in Matt. 24:15-22: He passed without a break from the Roman armies coming to destroy the Jewish nation, desolate the temple and Jerusalem to the Papal desolator of the Christian church. The same principle may also be seen by comparing Luke 21:24—the literal Romans "trod down" the literal "Jerusalem"—with Rev. 11:2 where the spiritual Romans were prophesied to "tread" "the holy city" "under foot forty and two months."

Prophecies in Isa. 13:19-22; Jer. 50; 51; etc., outlined the fall and subsequent desolation of ancient Babylon. The literal ruins are still visible to this day. Thus these prophecies are *still* meeting their *literal* fulfillment. However, the Revelation, the interpreter of Daniel's prophecies, applies these prophecies in a worldwide, antitypical sense.

The same principle governs every Old Testament prophecy dealing with events to transpire in the last days: they are *all* governed by the principle fully explained in the New Testament, that all the promises made to, and the prophecies concerning Israel and her land, now find their worldwide application in relation to the church. When national Israel was the chosen nation, and the land of Israel was her home and the place where God's blessings fell, then all the prophecies were interpreted literally, nationally, geographically: Israel, Jerusalem, the temple, and sacrifices were physical things in their midst. Israel's land was literal, and her enemies were literal, and their conflicts were fought with material swords. But the New Testament is explicit that these things are now applied spiritually in relation to the church, *though the language employed is precisely the same.* There is no change in the terminology employed, but there is a different application of the same words—they are spiritualized in relation to the church. The material, visible things, which were limited to the literal land and nation of Israel, *belonged to the Old Covenant.* The New Testament shows that the literal things of the Old Covenant have now *under the New Covenant,* a worldwide application. Especially since 1844, it has been possible to see more clearly the New Testament principle that the Old Testament things of Israel are lifted out of their literal, visible setting and applied in a worldwide application in relation to "the mysterious spiritual kingdom of which He spoke" (DA 391). Since 1844, light has shone more fully on the prophecies concerning "Israel." It may now be seen that the book of Revelation depicts the final conflict over the Sabbath and spiritual Israel, as if the church dwelt in the land of Israel and her foes gathered against her as she stands on Mt. Zion with Christ (Rev. 14:1, etc.). The Bible is not divided against itself. "The things revealed to Daniel were afterward *complemented* by the Revelation made to John on the Isle of Patmos. . . . Revelation . . . giving *fuller light* on the subjects dealt with in Daniel . . . they *both relate to the same subjects*" (TM 114-118). We are to "view the Word as a whole, and to see *the relation of its parts*" (Ed 190). "When thus searched out and brought together, they will be found to be *perfectly fitted to one another* . . . every prophecy an *explanation of another*" (Ed 123, 124). As the Revelation is an explanation of Daniel, the conflict which is presented in Daniel 11: 40-45, as occurring around Jerusalem, must be the same spiritual conflict which is portrayed around Jerusalem in the Revelation. "The Sabbath question is to be *the* issue in the great final conflict in which all the world will act a part" (6T 352). Those who apply the prophecies concerning Israel and the land of Israel in a literal, geographical sense do so as if the Old Covenant and the Palestinian aspect of the prophecies still applied.

By applying the New Testament principles that the church is now "the Israel of God," that all the Old Testament prophecies concerning Israel, the land of Israel, Jerusalem, Babylon, etc., now depict the experiences of the church and her enemies, we know that the prophecy concerning the kingdom of Babylon— the king of the north—could refer to nothing else than a description of the final conflict in which the church is attacked by the forces of Babylon, as described in the Revelation.

PRINCIPLE TWELVE:
"Double" and "Triple" Applications of Prophecy—"Rightly *Dividing* the Word of Truth" (2 Tim. 2:15)

It is vital for S.D.A. Bible students to be familiar with "double" and "triple" applications of prophecies concerning Israel and Jerusalem: without employing these essential principles the student will not be able to heed the Divine injunction to "rightly *divide*" the Word of truth. Failure to heed these principles lies at the foundation of many last-day errors, including those revealed in the "military" interpretation of Armageddon. The Bible is written on the principle of "multum in parvo," or much in little. It is a book written on definite principles, harmonizing logic with spiritual vision. The principles of enlargement by repetition, of the first things foreshadowing the last, the worldwide symbolized in the local things of the past, types and antitypes, past events "acted parables" of future things, "double" and "triple" applications, etc., prove that nothing in the Scripture is useless or wasted: that the past and the future are profitable for the present.

The principle of going back to where a thing commences and returning by means of a progressive cycle on an ascending scale, is clearly seen in Scripture and in nature. In the musical world, this principle is represented by the octave. The octave brings us back to begin again on the same note, but an octave higher. In the study of phyllotaxis—the branch or leaf arrangement of trees and plants—we find that each tree or plant has its normal mathematical number. Commencing with a certain branch or leaf, the stem is circled once, or more, according to the mathematical number of the tree, before the next branch or leaf appears directly above the one from which we commenced to count—and so on up the trunk or branch. Thus, on the spiral system, we recommence to count with the original number—only higher up the tree or plant. The principle of going back and commencing again by means of a progressive cycle is seen in the days of the week, the months of the year, the seasons, the revolutions of the moon around the earth, the earth around the sun, the sun around its central star, and in all the worlds revolving around the throne of God.

This principle so widely-employed in the economy of God—of going back to the commencement on a progressive, ascending scale—must not be overlooked in the interpretation of Bible prophecies, for God's ways are the same in nature and in His Word. Those things which are introduced in the early parts of the Bible are repeated and enlarged until, in the Revelation, they are employed *in a worldwide sense*. "In the Revelation all the books of the Bible meet and end" (AA 585). The Revelation provides the keys of interpretation for the understanding of all preceding books. The Revelation demonstrates principles upon which the whole Bible is written.

Even the casual reader of Holy Writ observes that the things appearing in the first chapters of Genesis re-appear on a grander scale in the last chapters of Revelation: In Genesis, before the inception of sin, we see a beginning of a new heaven and earth, a sinless paradise, a holy people, access to the tree of life, open communion with God. The Revelator, after sin has been banished from this world, concludes by describing the same conditions restored. In Genesis, Satan enters to deceive, man fears, and hides from God, is banished from the tree of life, Eden is lost, the gates are shut, the earth is cursed, pains, sorrows, tears, and death follow. The Revelation concludes the sacred Writings by pointing to the time when these conditions shall be removed. All that was lost in Eden is to be restored—in a richer, fuller way (PP 62). In these things, and in others that could be mentioned, is revealed the principle operating in the economy of God—the past is repeated, but on a vaster scale, a higher order. As things mentioned in the early chapters of the Bible are referred to in later books, so, similarly, things mentioned in the early chapters of the Revelation are later referred to and enlarged upon. The Second Advent, introduced in Rev. 1:7, is repeatedly brought to our attention throughout this Book until it is emblazoned in the chapters describing the final conflict.

PRINCIPLE THIRTEEN:
The Principle of the "Triple" Application Revealed in the Apocalypse

The Revelation deals with the past, present, and the future—see 1:19; 4:1. The things of ancient Israel are repeated, but on a vaster scale. The same terminology is employed throughout. However, a careful analysis reveals a different application before or after the second Advent. The term, "The holy city," of Dan. 9:24; Mat. 4:5; 27:53 (referring to the *literal* Jerusalem) is employed symbolically in Rev. 11:2 to refer to the church (GC 266). The same term "the holy city," mentioned in Rev. 21:2; 22:19, refers to the *literal* capital—the New Jerusalem—of the eternal kingdom. This illustrates the principle of the *triple* application of Scriptural terminology *of the things of Israel*: (1) *Literal* in relation to the literal Jews and the literal land of Israel; (2) *Symbolical* in relation to the spiritual kingdom of Christ; (3) *Literal* again when referring to the eternal kingdom of Christ. The term, "temple," designated the building in Jerusalem. In Rev. 11:1 the "temple" (in its earthly application) refers to the church. Other references in the Revelation to the "temple" refer to the temple in heaven where Christ pleads for His people. Thus again is revealed the triple use of that term: (1) *Literal* in the days of literal Israel; (2) *symbolical* in this—"dispensation of the Holy Spirit"; (3) *Literal* in the heavenly kingdom. Following the divinely-given principle of interpretation, we know that the words in Rev. 14:20, "And the winepress was trodden *without the city*," depict the slaughter of the wicked outside the *symbolic* city, the church, *before the millennium*, and the slaughter of the wicked outside the *literal* New Jerusalem *after the millennium* (Rev. 20:8, 9).

The Revelator applies Ezekiel's prophecy (Ezek. 38; 39) of the gathering of Gog's great armies against Israel (compare Rev. 19:17,

18 with Ezek. 39:17-20: Note the emphasis on the word *"place"* in Ezek. 39:11 and in Rev. 16:16) as the attempt of the world's forces to destroy God's remnant church. He interprets the gathering of Gog's army as a *symbolic* picture *before* the millennium. *After* the millennium He applies the prophecy to the *literal* gathering of Gog's armies (all the unsaved) against the *literal* city, the New Jerusalem (Rev. 20:8, 9). The time periods mentioned in the Revelation are intended to be understood *symbolically* until the Second Advent, after which the 1000 years is meant to be understood *literally*, see GC 659-661. There is a *symbolic* lake of fire (Rev. 19:20) before the 1000 years, but a *literal* lake of fire after the 1000 years (Rev. 20:10, 14, 15).

The Lord's servant says that "Christ is the Center of all true doctrine" (CT 453). Only as the many things of Israel mentioned in the prophecies of the Revelation are interpreted in relation to the Messiah's kingdom is it possible to make "Christ the Center of" these prophecies concerning Israel and the "Center" of the final conflict, which is portrayed as occurring in the land of Israel. But to make "Christ, the great center from which radiates all glory" (TM 19), it is necessary to interpret the prophetic presentations as a *symbolic* gathering *before* the Second Advent and a *literal* gathering *after* the 1000 years. That which was literal in relation to national Israel centered in literal Jerusalem is given its *"double,"* or *symbolic*, application in relation to Christ's *present* kingdom of *grace* centered in the *symbolic* Jerusalem, the church; and, *after the 1000 years, its "triple"* application—which is *literal*—in relation to the New Jerusalem. The same pictures which are *symbolically* applied *before* the Second Advent, have their *triple*—their final—application, in a *literal* sense, in connection with the *literal* New Jerusalem.

In harmony with this Biblical principle of interpretation, the Spirit of Prophecy applies such prophecies as Zech. 14, Joel 3, etc., *symbolically before* the millennium, and *literally after* the 1000 years. For instance, the Lord's servant applies Zech. 14:12, 13: the fate of those who have gathered and fought against Jerusalem, in connection with the fate of "the false shepherds" who have led the multitudes to make war against the remnant church (EW 289, 290; GC 657). This *symbolic* application, of course, is that given in Rev. 16:10. However, the Lord's servant, writing of events occurring *after* the 1000 years, presents a *literal* fulfillment of Zechariah's prophecy that the Messiah's "feet shall stand in that day upon the mount of Olives, which is before Jerusalem on the east . . . and there shall be a very great valley," see GC 663; EW 291.

The Lord's servant, ever faithful in following the principles of interpretation given in the Revelation, has applied this same principle of interpretation in referring to Joel's prophecy, which portrays the gathering of the nations, or "heathen" (same word in the Hebrew) against God's people in Jerusalem. God declares that their preparations to make war upon His people will lead them to their doom, for He will judge them for their persecution of His people: "Assemble yourselves, and come, all ye heathen [or nations], and gather yourselves together *round about* . . . for there will I sit to judge all the heathen *round about*" (3:11, 12). The Spirit of Prophecy applies this gathering of the "heathen" (or nations) *"round about"* God's people in Jerusalem (see Joel 3:32) as a *symbolic* presentation of the final conflict in which the "heathen" threaten to destroy the remnant church. At that time, God's people pray: "Make a way of escape for Thy people! *Deliver* us from the heathen *round about us*. . . . Soon I heard the voice of God which shook the heavens and the earth (Joel 3:16). . . . Their captivity was turned. . . . Their enemies, *the heathen around them*, fell like dead men" (1T 183, 184). After the 1000 years, when describing the literal gathering of the unsaved— "the armies of Satan"—with literal "implements of war" against the literal "city of God," the Lord's servant borrows words from Joel's prophecy when she says: "He [Satan] makes the *weak strong* [see Joel 3:10] and inspires all with his own spirit" (GC 663, 664). Thus it will be readily seen that the gathering of the "heathen," the nations, *"round about"* God's people *in Jerusalem* is employed *symbolically* by God's servant when writing of the attack upon the remnant church; but when she wrote of events occurring after the 1000 years, she stated: "The armies of Satan *surround* ['*round about*'] the city, and make ready for the onset." Thus, again, we see how the Lord's servant applies *symbolically* the prophecies which depict the combined forces of the world against the remnant, and then applies those same prophecies in a *literal* application after the 1000 years.

Through the Revelation and the Spirit of Prophecy, the Lord has shown the principle to be employed in "rightly *dividing*" the Apocalypse *and other parts of the Holy Scriptures*. The millennium is the dividing line between the application of the *symbolical* and the application of the *literal*, just as the cross and the rejection of the Jewish nation terminated the literal, national, typical system and introduced the period of the antitypical, spiritual church application. The Apocalypse is a revelation of the whole Bible, and shows the true interpretation of all that pertains to Israel—past, present, and future. The prophecies of Ezekiel, Daniel, Zechariah, Joel, etc., should be interpreted in harmony with the principle of the triple application of the things of Israel so clearly revealed in the Revelation. It is far beyond the limited scope of this brief outline to begin to show how the triple application enters into the warp and the woof of the design of many passages of the sacred Scriptures. Failure to apply this principle has prevented some from "rightly dividing the Word of truth."

In the Revelation, the storm center of the ages is the city of Jerusalem, the name of which means "foundations of peace"; Jerusalem, the city of "the Prince of Peace." To correctly understand the Revelation, Jerusalem must be interpreted as the center of the battle between good and evil. In the Old Testament, Jerusalem was the center of national Israel, and many of Israel's national enemies came against Jerusalem. These enemies are brought into the symbolical imagery of the Revelation as types of the enemies who gather around Jerusalem to attack God's people. The Revelation carries this representation through until the end of the 1000 years: then, *all* the literal enemies of ancient Israel and *all* the enemies of the church will literally gather around the literal city in which reigns the visible Son of God, the Prince of Peace, the Destroyer of the evil which makes "war" upon Him, and on His people. In the prophecy of Joel, as in other prophecies of the Bible depicting the conflict between good and evil, Jerusalem is the center. In Joel 2:32, deliverance from the foes without the city is vouchsafed to "the remnant" within Jerusalem. This was literally true in the history of national Israel (see 2 Kings 18:17-37; Isa. 37:32-36, etc.) when they were faithful to God. This prophecy portrays symbolically the protection, the deliverance, of God's "remnant" people in the final conflict; and this same prophecy envisages the deliverance of all God's people in the New Jerusalem at the end of the 1000 years. As the triple application of the prophecies concerning Israel become clearer to the student of Holy Writ, he discerns more of the wonderful wisdom of God in the design thus revealed in the Scriptures, and he rejoices in receiving a better understanding of the prophecies depicting the final conflict, which causes him to find rest and comfort in knowing that "God will in a wonderful manner preserve His people through the time of trouble" (1T 353).

Any one of the foregoing principles is sufficient to establish our faith in God's last-day message. However, when the Message is studied in the light of all the principles herein presented, the Message is seen to be based upon an irrefragible foundation. There are other principles which lack of space will not permit in this outline, but these only confirm the truths herein expressed. For a perfect balance in understanding God's last-day Message there must be a harmonious application of all the laws of interpretation. These laws supplement each other and provide a checking system whereby the student of Holy Writ is able to be positive that his understanding of certain passages is in harmony with the rest of Scripture. These principles of interpretation must all blend together as do the colors of the foundations of the New Jerusalem, and this they do when the Bible is left to explain itself. Salvation is not dependent upon a scholarly appreciation of the laws of interpretation, but is dependent upon "repentance toward God, and faith toward our Lord Jesus Christ." However, those who love God and desire to do His will be led to think the thoughts of God after Him, and will be led by the Holy Spirit "into all truth."

The following titles by Louis F. Were are also available:

144,000 Sealed: When? Why?
The Certainty of the Third Angel's Message
Christ the Center
Christ's Last Message to His Remnant
The Fire of His Jealousy
The King of the North at Jerusalem
The Kings That Come From the Sunrising
The Life Triumphant
The Moral Purpose of Prophecy
The Truth Concerning Mrs. E. G. White, Uriah Smith, and the King of the North
The Woman and the Beast in the Book of Revelation

To order any of these titles by Louis F. Were, or for a free catalog of books, videos, audio tapes and more at discount prices, contact:

Laymen Ministries
414 Zapada Rd.
St. Maries, ID 83861-9403

Phone: (208) 245-5388
Fax: (208) 245-3280
Toll free order line: 1-800-245-1844
email: office@lmn.org
      lmbookstore@lmn.org
Visit our website at www.lmn.org

Laymen Ministries is a self-supporting, privately funded 501 (c)(3) nonprofit corporation. We exist to encourage lay people in all parts of the world that, through being empowered by the Holy Spirit, they are the working force of the church, and are called to proclaim the Three Angels' Messages in our generation. It is our aim to help provide the necessary tools to accomplish this goal—to educate in practical religion, provide health education, assist in publication and distribution of literature, video, audio, and other media productions, etc. More information on our current international projects is available by contacting our office. Tax deductible receipts for donations are issued monthly.

An Adventist Apocalypse

By Ellen G. White

A compilation of hundreds of quotations from unpublished letters and manuscripts covering a wide range of issues and events that will confront the people of God in the last days. Much of this material is previously unreleased, nowhere else to be found.

This is a paperback edition with easy to read type. Learn what God's messenger had to say about preparing for the coming conflict, the working of the enemy, the Latter Rain, events preceding the Second Coming, the Loud Cry, what will happen within the church, how God will sustain His children, the Judgment... and too many more topics to list. 160 pages.

Retail Price: $9.95 **Discount Price: $8.45** + S&H

The Sanctuary Series

Five *Sanctuary* volumes under one cover

By Arla Van Etten

Each detail of Type (earthly sanctuary) and Antitype (heavenly sanctuary) is presented side by side in an easily understood format, with texts and references for study. Designed for youth, but with ample content to provide adults with a fascinating, in-depth study, as well. Great for study groups!

240 pages, paperback.

This edition contains:

The Young People's Sanctuary Series

    Volume 1: The Camp Around

    Volume 2: The Courtyard

    Volume 3: The Offerings

    Volume 4: The Tent Tabernacle

    Volume 5: The Holy Days and Feast Days

Retail Price: $~~17.95~~ **Discount Price: $16.50** + S&H

Bible Students' Library

The Bible Students' Library series was originally published between 1889 and 1905, and was written by the Adventist pioneers. These booklets clearly present the principles of our faith. Excellent for your own study or for a witnessing tool. Most are under 30 pages and priced under $1.00, and all are small enough to fit in a pocket or purse. Additional savings when bought in lots of 100 or more.

Titles included:

Baptism, Its Significance, by E. J. Waggoner

Bible Sanctification, by

Can We Keep the Sabbath? by E. J. Waggoner

Christ Tempted As We Are, by Ellen G. White

The Full Assurance of Faith, by E. J. Waggoner

Home Missionary Work, by Ellen G. White

The Immortality of the Soul, by A.T. Jones

The Judgment: The Waymarks to the Holy City, by James White

Justified by Faith, by Ellen G. White

Living by Faith, by E. J. Waggoner

The Lost Time Questions, by J. H. Waggoner

Privilege of Prayer, by Ellen G. White

The Prophetic Gift in the Gospel Church, by J. N. Loughborough

The Relation of the Law to the Gospel, by F. C. Gilbert

The Sabbath in Prophecy, by W. H. Littlejohn

The Second Advent Its Manner, Object & Nearness, by James White

The Sufferings of Christ, by Ellen G. White

Sunday: The Origin of Its Observance in the Christian Church, by E. J. Waggoner

The Sure Foundation & the Keys of the Kingdom, by E. J. Waggoner

Order securely online at www.lmn.org • Toll free order line: (800) 245-1844

Apples of Gold Library

Also written by the Adventist pioneers and published between 1893 and 1905 as tracts especially designed to fit in an envelope for mailing to friends and family. These little gems are excellent for your own study and for distribution in literature racks, or for evangelism and personal witnessing.

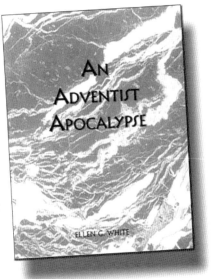

Only $.30 each, or $.20 each for 100 or more.

Title included:

The Christian's Privilege,
    by Ellen G. White

The Elect of God, by Ellen G. White

The Father's Duty, by Ellen G. White

Foreknowledge & Foreordination,
    by E. J. Waggoner

God's Word the Parent's Guide, by Ellen G. White

Home Training—Its Importance & Results, by Ellen G. White

Hope in Trials, by Ellen G. White

How to Get Knowledge, by E. J. Waggoner

The Power of Forgiveness, by E. J. Waggoner

The Power of the Word, by Ellen G. White

The Responsibility of Parents, by Ellen G. White

Salvation in Jesus Christ, by E. J. Waggoner

Three Sabbaths, by E. J. Waggoner

What Must I Do to Be Saved?, by Ellen G. White

Order securely online at www.lmn.org • Toll free order line: (800) 245-1844

Who is Laymen Ministries?

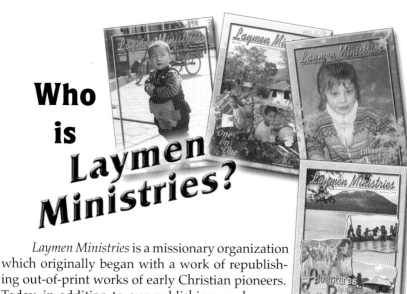

Laymen Ministries is a missionary organization which originally began with a work of republishing out-of-print works of early Christian pioneers. Today, in addition to our publishing work, we also train and equip laymen in many parts of the world in translation and publishing of materials that will help spread the news of God's great love and Jesus' soon return. We have a video production facility which provides programming for videos, satellite TV broadcast, and culturally adapted materials in their native languages for 3rd world countries. We also support media and broadcast ministries in these countries, and the training of laymen as pastors, Bible workers, and literature evangelists, as well as providing medical outreach and life-style training to help people live happier, healthier lives.

If you would like to learn more about the work we do, and about some of the fascinating projects we are involved in, please contact our office to receive your FREE subscription to our magazine, which contains exciting mission updates, as well as timely articles to strengthen and encourage laymen in all walks of life. We also offer a catalog with hundreds of books, videos, audios, and more at discount prices! Our catalog is also available online for your shopping convenience.

(208) 245-5388 • Toll free order line: (800) 245-1844
email: **office@lmn.org** • **lmbookstore@lmn.org**
Order securely online at **www.lmn.org**